# *Praises for Afghan Cuisine*

Amazon.com reviews:

**WOW!!! Wonderful Recipes!!,** "If you have ever had afghan food, it doesn't seem very easy to make. This book makes it so simple and it will be the tastiest food you have ever had! I have only tried a few of the dishes and each one has come out tasting so authentic and delicious. My favorite so far is the potato borani and the Khorshaid's chicken. I definitely recommend this book to anyone from the most experienced to the most inexperienced (like me) cooks out there!" --Anonymous reader, California

**I definitely recommend this book!** "This book made it really easy to follow the recipes. Also, knowing that the proceeds give back to Afghanistan is important because having gone there, I know they need a lot of support to pick themselves up. It's great that this book helps to give back!" --Annette Golding, Virginia

**Wonderful Addition to my Cookbook Collection** "Both my mother and I have thoroughly enjoyed this book…I cooked [Qabli] rice and it was DELICIOUS!! My uncle LOVED the rice when he tasted it. This cookbook has many wonderful recipes and the author of the book is also just as wonderful. From reading this book, I feel like I have gotten to know her and taste Afghan food through her senses. I recommend this book to everyone".

**Delicious Afghan recipes in easy-to-follow steps** "A real find for anyone who's wanted to duplicate distinctive Afghan dishes! Contains traditional food I've only eaten in restaurants...Steps are easy to follow, even for novice cooks like me. And it's gratifying that the author plans to send a portion of the proceeds to help Afghani women and children". --Anonymous reader

**Great book with useful recipes** "This is a great book with useful authentic recipes that are easy to use. The food is delicious and the recipes make it easy to make the dishes at home. I highly recommend this book for anyone wanting to experience yummy Afghan food but don't want to follow complicated recipes. I also love the fact that this book also includes non Afghan recipes".

–Anonymous reader, California

**Deceptively simple--wonderfully delicious!** "When I started reading through the recipes in this book, I thought: "These are too simple! Not enough spices, not enough ingredients. This will probably come out bland!" How wrong I was! A potato dish (last night's dinner) called for only 6 ingredients (including spices!), was incredibly simple to make, and came out wonderfully fragrant and flavorful. The quarmas (meat dishes) I've made have likewise been easy to shop for and cook, but have been incredibly satisfying. For the bold cook, there ARE some more challenging recipes, such as complex chalau (pilaf/biriyani) dishes. But for those seeking a simple, tasty introduction to a new style of cuisine, I highly recommend this book!" --Akash J, Virginia

## E-mailed feedback:

"I wanted to congratulate you for such a nice book you wrote, 'Afghan Cuisine - Cooking for Life'. It is amazing that you were able to put it together in such an easy to understand, simple format. See, I too love to cook...currently though I can't cook. I live in a military barracks on the outskirts of Kabul...There isn't the space in my room to cook and I really miss it. I bought your book so that I could dream about cooking and talk to my interpreter about what all the ingredients are (I'm a dork - I take notes and all). I also wanted a book so that we can discuss the dishes and he can go out and get them (travel for us is still unsafe and somewhat limited). So every so often we eat and I can check off in your book what I've eaten - this way it will help me get the whole experience here...Your ideas about helping the Afghan people are similar to a lot of ours. We spend a lot of time handing out "stuff" to kids from pencils and notebooks to athletic equipment. Also, we run medical missions to provide care for those who don't get what they need. We have even "adopted" a local town, Tangikaly, just to our east, to help out in as many ways as we can...looking forward to getting home and using some of those recipes - and maybe writing my own cookbook one day!

--Andy, Afghanistan

"I am very much enjoying your book and always turn to it for any cooking advice".

--Lucy Poduskova, United Kingdom

"I have recently purchased your cookbook and have tried some of the recipes. Thank you so much for publishing this book. We really needed a book like this. Your recipes are easy to follow and they turn out great...I am an Afghan who does not enjoy cooking but loves food especially Afghan. With your book, I have been able to make some of the dishes without the usual fuss".

--Fauzia, Southern CA

"This January my husband and my stepdaughter presented me with your cookbook. I had seen Middle Eastern cookbooks, but never one devoted only to Afghan recipes. What a wonderful surprise it was to receive your book! (I believe they found it on Amazon)...I decided to start with a recipe that seemed easy, so I made the basic ground beef meat sauce and served it over basmati rice boiled on the stovetop in the way I am accustomed to preparing it. The meal turned out very well. Next I decided to tackle the Qabli Palau. I have had this dish at the restaurant, so I felt I would be able to compare the result. I was quite nervous about making this recipe, as I was sure, with so little liquid, I would end up with a pot of burned rice (either that or, if I added more liquid during the cooking, I would have a risotto instead of a palau!) Since I cannot control the burners on my stove that well, after soaking and boiling the rice for 3 minutes, I drained the rice and decided to put the whole thing in the oven at 300 degrees for about 30 minutes. I have to say, I think it worked! The rice was not sticky at all, was loose and dry, and was slightly al dente. The result was comparable to [the restaurant] palau and my husband loved it... Thanks so much for your wonderful cookbook. I have read it cover-to-cover several times (really!) We will continue to visit [our favorite restaurant] because the people are so nice, the food is so good, and the Afghan decorations are quite beautiful. It will be great fun, however, to prepare these recipes at home! I was glad to read that some of the proceeds from the book are going to the women and children of Afghanistan. It is my sincerest hope that peace will come soon to your native land and that its people and culture will once again thrive."

--Karin, Philadelphia

# Afghan Cuisine

# Afghan Cuisine

*A Collection of Family Recipes*

*Nafisa Sekandari*

*Avagana Publishing*
*Fremont, CA*

Afghan Cuisine by Nafisa Sekandari



*Edition ISBNs*

| | |
|---|---|
| 2nd Edition | 978-0615361314 (Avagana Publishing, 2010) |
| First Edition | 978-1403385904 (Author house, 2003) |

Library of Congress Control Number: 2002095170

| | |
|---|---|
| Photos: | Nafisa Sekandari |
| Cover: | Jason Maraccini |
| Interior: | Elysia Shaw |
| Logo: | Felicia Gold |

Printed in the United States of America

Author in Herat, 2003

## *Table of Contents*

# Forward

I began the task of revising "Afghan Cuisine" immediately after it was published in 2002 and have since marked up my personal copy of the book with numerous hand written notes. I wanted to revise and re-publish this book after having adapted and revised the recipes over the years. I've since simplified some of the recipes, added new recipes, and corrected others.

I was a complete novice in the kitchen when the first edition of Afghan Cuisine was published. As a result, I was afraid to experiment and was very rigid about following recipes. In the previous edition, I was simply taking recipes and formatting them in an easy to use process without checking for the accuracy of the recipes. When obtaining recipes that have been in the family for years, I found it difficult to rely on their accuracy. At the time, my lack of cooking skills also prevented me from seeing the blatant errors in the recipes. I have since grown in my cooking abilities and am able to not only recognize the errors but modify the recipes to my liking. Family members that have been cooking all their lives are used to estimating the amount of ingredients and very few utilize measuring instruments in their cooking. For this reason, every family has their distinct version of each recipe. There is no hard and fast rule to follow.

When I initially took on the task of compiling family recipes in a cookbook, I was unaware of the tremendous need for a book like this in the Afghan community. I was writing a book for my personal use, not knowing thousands of people around the world would be using the book as a reference in their own kitchens. At the time of publication, I was unprepared for the success of this book. Therefore, I felt obligated to go through the recipes in the first edition with a fine toothed comb to ensure all the recipes were not only authentic, but also easy for beginners.

Over the past few years, I've become very health and environmentally conscious. I focus on reducing my carbon footprint on the world and reducing, reusing, and recycling whenever I can. With the birth of my daughter, I've also switched to eating whole, unprocessed, mostly organic foods. I was pleasantly surprised to find that Afghan cuisine can easily accommodate this lifestyle change. Inherently, Afghan food is very healthy and nutritious with much of the ingredients containing numerous health benefits. I have listed some of the benefits of many of the spices used in the herbs and spices chapter.

## *Giving Back*

Many often ask me about how the book helped me raise money for charity. At the time of the initial publication of the book, I had big dreams of raising enough money from book royalties to help the women and children in Afghanistan. Unfortunately, the royalties earned from the sales of the first edition were not large enough to realize the fundraising goals I had had, but that didn't stop me from making my own personal contributions to those charities. I support several charitable organizations that deal with meeting the needs of women and children both in and out of Afghanistan. I will continue to support these charities, regardless of the profits I make from this book. Women and children continue to suffer in many parts of the world, but those in Afghanistan are near and dear to my heart and I want to do all I can in supporting them. Based on a recent study, Afghanistan has the worst primary education rate for females in the world as well as the lowest female life expectancy, and the highest levels of infant mortality rate.

If you would like to contribute to some of the charitable organizations I support, please contact:

| **The Children of War**<br><br>P.O. Box 223602<br>Chantilly, VA 20153 | Sarahim Center for Afghan Children with Disabilities<br><br>13835 N. Tatum Blvd. #624<br>Phoenix, AZ 85032<br><br>www.sarahimcenter.org | Sana Orphanage<br><br>P. O. Box 68248<br>Seattle WA 98168<br>206.972.8886<br><br>www.sanaorphanage.org |
|---|---|---|
| UNICEF USA<br><br>www.unicefusa.org | Islamic Relief<br><br>P.O. Box 5640<br>Buena Park, CA 90622<br>1(888) 479-4968<br><br>www.islamicreliefusa.org | CARE<br><br>151 Ellis St. NE<br>Atlanta, GA 30303<br><br>www.my.care.org |

*This book is dedicated to my sweet daughter. May these recipes help you as much as they have helped me in my journey of learning to cook Afghan food.*

## *Acknowledgements*

I want to thank my daughter for her patience during the revision process of this book

I'm deeply grateful to my father for going over every recipe and revising and editing along with me. He has always been a huge supporter of whatever project I'm working on and yet again has come through in his support. He never ceases to amaze me in his depth of knowledge and experience, regardless the topic. Thank you to my sister Nelofer and my cousin Hosai for their contributions in the editing process of this book.

I continue to be grateful for the generosity of my mother and relatives in sharing their recipes with me.

I'm grateful to Jason Maraccini for developing the cover and being so patient with my many requests for changes and revisions. I'm also grateful to Elysia Shaw for providing me with such great interior designs for the chapters. Elysia is a high school student with great potential for success in the design field in the future. Thanks also to Felicia Gold, a high school student with great talent, for the great logo design.

I'd like to thank everyone who has purchased this book and provided me with feedback and encouragement via emails from around the world. This book has helped me as much as it has helped those who have purchased it. I refer to it frequently and credit the book for helping me gain confidence in the kitchen.

# About Afghanistan

Afghanistan is a totally landlocked country about the size of Texas, with an extremely rugged topography. It borders Iran, Turkmenistan, Uzbekistan, Tajikistan, China, and Pakistan. Afghanistan's location is strategically important to all the surrounding countries.

The country is home to beautiful mountain ranges, strikingly crystal clear rivers, and dry dusty desserts. In the northeast part of the country, the highest peak of the mountains reaches 24,600 ft.

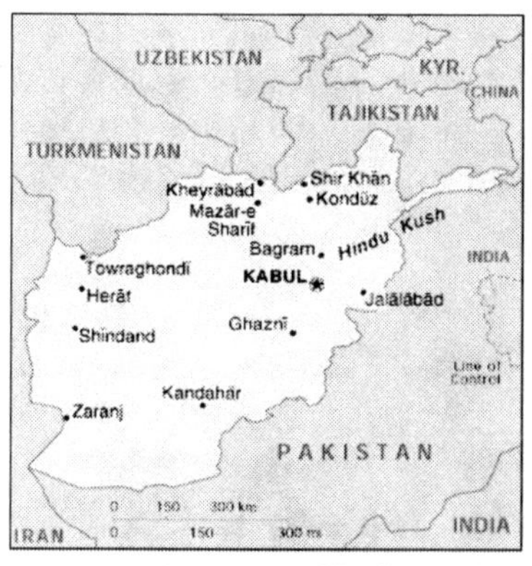


America's involvement in Afghanistan since 2001 has kept the country in the media spotlight and has attracted a lot of attention to the culture and its people. Americans know more about Afghanistan today than they did a decade ago. It was because of this coverage that Afghanistan has undergone such drastic changes over the past several years. Today the majority of Afghans have access to television programs not only from Afghanistan but from around the world. Most have access to the internet and cellular phones. Afghans more than ever are now exposed to Western culture, music, and food. There is currently one Westernized shopping mall in the country which is located in the capital city of Kabul.

Many of these changes occurred after my trip to Afghanistan in 2003. At that time, the effects of war were painfully visible at every turn. Upon our landing in Kabul airport, I began sobbing uncontrollably after seeing the broken airplanes littering the area. My heart broke for the suffering my country had been witness to.

*My grandmother's house reduced to just a shell*

The crumbling infrastructure could be seen all over the city of Kabul. In my hometown of Herat, bullets riddled the walls of my elementary school as well as the home I grew up in. Old Russian tanks could be seen underneath piles of dirt.

*The house I grew up in with bullet ridden walls*

*Building in Kabul, 2003*

Kabul, the capital city, used to be a bustling city prior to the Soviet invasion of 1979. Today Kabul has little remaining from its historic past. The majority of historical landmarks have been destroyed over the 30 year period of war. In my trip I wished there were "before" and "after" photos of the landmarks so I could see what the city used to look like. As a child I used to hear about the beauty of Kabul and the surrounding cities but there was very little beauty to be seen in 2003. The exception was the crystal clear blue sky as well as the beautiful mountain tops, visible from the city.

*Downtown Kabul, 2003*

*On our way to Salang, 2003*

Despite the war, hospitality and guests remain very important to the Afghan people. Even though the people living in Afghanistan had very little to eat themselves, they continued to share what little they had with guests. This is because hospitality and guests are a very important part of the Muslim religion. With Afghans and Muslims, there is always an open door policy regarding guests. Afghan food is a big part of the tradition and custom of Afghanistan. It is the center of every family gathering and the main part of social occasions.

Afghan food is a blend of cooking styles from Iran and India as well as from the many groups of invaders that invaded and occupied Afghanistan throughout the centuries. The spices used in Afghan food create a taste unlike the food of the surrounding countries. The food is neither bland nor spicy hot. There is a wonderful blend of taste and aroma.

Afghan specialties include Palau and kabobs. Quarma's (sauces) are served with Chalau (white basmati rice). Tea is an important part of Afghan dining and is served after every meal. Afghans usually drink black tea with cardamom but the trend in the United States is changing to green tea. Sweets are often a perfect companion to tea. Noqul (chickpeas or almonds covered with sugar and spices) and Qand (sugar cubes) are usually served to guests at family gatherings and weddings. There are also a variety of cookies, pastries, and candies.

Afghan bread (Naan) is a major staple in the life of Afghans. Afghan bread is very versatile and can be used for breakfast, lunch, or dinner. The bread resembles a long pizza without the toppings. Afghans in the United States used to bake their own bread but due to the major effort it requires to make the bread and the wide availability of the bread in Afghan grocery stores today, many choose to simply buy it. Warm, fresh out of the oven Afghan bread is especially irresistible to even the most bread-phobic individual.

*Girl carrying bread on her head, Kabul 2003*

Afghans traditionally include meat in most of their recipes. The meat used can be lamb or beef. Afghans, being Muslim, do not eat pork or pork products. The meat is usually "halal" which means that the animal needs to be slaughtered a certain way. In the Muslim manner, that means that a prayer asking God for permission ("In the name of God the most compassionate, the most merciful") is said prior to slaughtering the animal at the throat. This is believed to be the best way to drain the blood and prevent bacterial growth and the most painless and humane way for the animal to die.

*Bala e-sar, Kabul 2003*

Getting
Started

The organization of the recipes in this book is intended to be easy to follow. This book is not meant to be a traditional Afghan cookbook. There are many traditional home style Afghan cookbooks out there, but I wanted mine to incorporate cultural influences from the West while at the same time speak to the in learning how to cook Afghan food in a simple manner. All of the recipes I have listed in this book attempt to keep the goal of healthy eating intact.

For variety, I have also included many nontraditional dishes that have become my favorites over the years. Having lived in the United States now for over 30 years, we have naturally been exposed to foods from diverse backgrounds. In our exposure, we, as you would expect, have adopted various recipes into our cuisine. Afghan cuisine by its history is a mixture of dishes from surrounding regions so it's only natural to continue to expand our recipes. Although it is the intention of most Afghans to retain the traditional recipes of Afghanistan, we have to accept the reality that our recipes have been influenced by our new home in the United States.

Traditional Afghan cooking gets its rich flavor from using large amounts of oil in some dishes, but where possible, I reduced the amount of oil required in my recipe adaptations. You can adjust the amount of oil for your own taste as well. Afghan food can be low in fat and still delicious. Traditional Afghan cooking can also be difficult to pick up for beginners here in the United States due to time and ingredient accessibility. For this cookbook, I take traditional recipes, and while retaining the traditional flavor, include some short cuts and common ingredients that are easily found here in the West.

Afghan cooking takes practice and patience. Not too many dishes can be prepared in a rush. The quarma's take time but the ingredients can be tempered with to suit individual tastes. My spice measurements might be too much or not enough depending on the individual. I've learned to play with the measurements and put in what I think is enough, but occasionally I see my mom put in more than I would but the food always comes out good. So don't be afraid. After a few times of cooking, you will strike a perfect balance and be able to "put in a little bit of this and a pinch of that".

Although experienced Afghan cooks typically don't use measuring instruments in their cooking, I thought I'd include a reference for the rest of us.

***Measurements***

3 teaspoons = 1 tablespoon=15 ml.
4 tablespoons = ¼ cup
5 ½ tablespoons= ½ cup
16 tablespoons= 1 cup
2 ounce = ¼ cup
1 cup = 8 ounces
4 cups = 1 quart
4 quarts = 1 gallon
16 ounce (2 cups) = 1 pound=.4536 kilograms
1 gal=4 qt=8pt=16 cup=128 fl oz. =3.79 liter
½ gal=2qt=4 pt=8cup=64 fl. oz. =1.89 liter
¼ gal=1 qt=2 pt=4 cup=32 fl. oz. = .95 liter
½ qt=1 pt=2 cup=16 fl. oz. = .47 liter
¼ qt= ½ pt=1 cup=8 fl. oz. = .24 liter

9-10 egg whites = 1 cup
1 pound of dry rice = 2 cups of dry rice = 6 cups of cooked rice
1 pound of sugar = 2 ¼ cups
1 pound of dry beans = 2 dry cups of dry beans = 6 cups of cooked beans

## ***Time Saving Tips***

- Frying large quantities of sliced onions ahead of time and freezing it saves a lot of time in dishes such as Quarma, Aush, Kitchiree Quroot, and Palau. You can use what you need as you need it. Store bought fried onions can also be used as a substitute.
- Mincing large quantities of garlic in a food processor and freezing it also saves a lot of time. I store mine in glass jars and use what I need and store in the freezer. I don't like the store bought variety due to added preservatives and taste. You can buy a container of peeled garlic from stores for mincing and freezing.
- Preparing the quarma base (yakhnee) in advance and storing in the freezer can save you time. You can thaw out what you need to make various quarma recipes in no time.
- Preparing large quantities of various quarma dishes and storing in the freezer comes in very handy for those occasions when you are short on time or have unexpected guests dropping by as is common in the Afghan culture.
- Pressure cookers are fantastic in reducing cooking time for dishes such as Shoula, Kitchiree quroot, quarmas, and soup.
- The Chinese pasta wraps are great substitutes for dough in such dishes as Aushak, Boulani, and Mantu. There are different variations available at the local grocery stores such as: Large square pasta wraps (eggroll wrappers) used for Boulani, small square pasta wraps (wonton wrappers) used for Mantu, and round pasta wraps (pot stickers and dumpling wrappers) used for Aushak.

Oil & Fat: I use only extra virgin, cold pressed olive oil in my cooking (with the exception of frying) but other oils such as canola oil and safflower oil work well also. I don't try and avoid fat in my cooking. Our bodies require healthy fats in order to function properly. Avoid saturated fats and partially hydrogenated oils but do incorporate healthy fats such as olive oil and omega 3 essential fatty acids (fish, walnuts, flax seeds) in your cooking and overall diet. Afghan food can be prepared using healthy fats such as olive oil. We also eat a lot of nuts in our diet which is a very good source of the healthy fatty acids.

Meats: When cooking with meat, I tend to use mostly chicken & turkey because they are lean meats and are high in protein. While some recipes in this book call for beef or lamb, in many cases chicken and turkey can be used as a substitute.

Pots: Afghan cooking comes out best in good quality pots and pans. The pots do not need to be expensive but should be good quality and heavy duty. I try and avoid non-stick pots due to the health risks involved. Also when using nonstick pots, you won't get the best "ty-digi" (the crust on the bottom of the pot of rice) once it's cooked.

Pressure Cooker: The new pressure cooker is not like the scary pressure cookers of the past. I used to fear pressure cookers but now I love using mine for many different dishes. I have stopped using canned beans and often rely on my pressure cooker to cook up dried beans in a hurry. There are many advantages to using a pressure cooker: Food cooks up to 70% faster in a pressure cooker and due to the shorter cooking time, more of the nutrients are retained. Pressure cookers save you time when wanting to make a quick meal for your family. I can put together a healthy nutritious meal in under 30 minutes.

# Herbs&Spices

## plus common ingredients

## ***Herbs and Spices most commonly used in Afghan Cooking***

*Afghan cooking uses many herbs and spices that are full of nutrients and have health benefits. Afghan food is not hot like Indian cuisine but it's also not bland. The spices add a lot of flavor to the food but do not overpower the dishes. Most of these herbs and spices can easily be found in your local grocery store or health food stores. The herbs and spices that are specific to the Afghan/Asian region can usually be found in Afghan, Iranian, or Indian grocery stores.*

**Anise (*Bodiyan*)**: Anise is used in many Afghan dishes but is also boiled to relieve digestive disorders. It is also commonly used to help with colic in infants, reduce stomach cramping, and thin out the mucous related to coughing.

**Basil Seeds** *(Raihan)*: These little seeds can be found in Afghan grocery stores or you can extract the seeds from the basil plant. Basil seeds are very beneficial for constipation, indigestion and heartburn. For the basil seed drink recipe, see page 27.

**Black Pepper** *(Murch-e-sia)*: Used in most afghan cooking. The alkaloid found in pepper stimulates the saliva and gastric juices, killing bacteria, improving the appetite, aiding digestion, reducing flatulence, and nausea. Black pepper is also good for digestive disorders.

**Black Seeds/Black Caraway Seeds (*Sia Dona*)**: Caraway seeds are used in various dishes, cookies, Rhote, and bread. These black seeds are also used to aid in digestion and good for treating stomach and intestinal problems along with migraines and high blood pressure. In the Arab culture, it is believed black seeds are a cure for all diseases except death.

**Cardamom** (*Hail*): Used in rice dishes, desserts, and tea. Cardamom has a cooling effect on the body and considered beneficial for mental alertness and digestive disorders.

**Cinnamon** (*Dal Chini*): Used in rice dishes, quarmas, and desert. Cinnamon has many health benefits including regulating blood sugar, lowering LDL cholesterol, and providing arthritis relief when combined with honey. Cinnamon is also a natural food preservative.

**Cloves** *(Mikhak*): Used in Palau and other dishes. Cloves are a nutrient dense spice and an excellent source of vitamin C and Omega 3 fatty acid. In addition to being considered a powerful antiseptic and anti-bacterial, it also has anti-inflammatory benefits.

**Coriander** *(Gashneez):* Coriander is ground cilantro seeds and is one of the main spices in most Afghan dishes. Coriander is often used to aid digestion and is an anti-inflammatory treatment for arthritis.

**Cumin** *(Zeera*): Used in Chalau and Palau. Said to be good for iron absorption. Used mostly in ground form unless specified. For Chalau, whole cumin is mixed with the rice right before it's steamed.

**Dill** *(Shibit):* Used in soups, rice dishes, and spinach quarmas. The list of benefits for dill is long but some of the benefits are aid in digestion, relief from insomnia, hiccups, diarrhea, dysentery, menstrual disorders, and respiratory disorders.

**Fenugreek (***Holba*): Used in spinach quarma. Fenugreek has many health benefits, mostly associated with hormonal balance, arthritis, asthma, and digestion. It is commonly used as a tea for new mothers interested in increasing their breast milk.

**Garlic** *(Seer*): Used in most Afghan dishes, including marinades, and tourshies. The health benefits of garlic are too numerous to list here but one of its benefits are a stronger immune system.

**Ginger** (*Zanjafeel*): Used ground or fresh in various dishes. Ginger has a warming effect on the stomach and used to soothe indigestion.

**Green Chili Peppers** *(Murch-e-sabz*): (Green chili Peppers, also known as jalapeno's (fat green peppers) or Serrano Peppers (thin, long green peppers). The green chilis are used in salads, soups, quarma's, chutneys, and tourshies (pickled vegetables).

**Gundana** (no English equivalent available): Long flat leaves that look like long grass. Gundana is difficult to find in the United States; unless you grow your own, which my mom did using seeds she bought from an Afghan store. If you can't find Gundana, you can substitute leeks or scallions instead in recipes. Used fresh in Aushak, Boulani, or salads.

**Mint** *(Nahna*): Used fresh or dry (crushed) in dishes, salads, and yogurt. Mint is known to aid in digestion and has a cooling effect on the stomach.

**Poppy Seeds** *(Khosh-Khosh*): The seeds are sprinkled on breads and cookies. Poppy seeds have many health benefits including but not limited to aid for indigestion, asthma, insomnia, and nausea.

**Red Chili Peppers** *(Murch-e-surkh):* The Red chilies are either fresh or dried, and are used whole, crushed, or ground. Red chilies are usually used for tourshies and quarmas.

**Pennyroyal** *(Pudina)*: A wild herb grown in Afghanistan, and used like crushed dried mint and sprinkled over Aushak, Aush, and yogurt. There are many health benefits to pudina including relief for headaches, colic, colds, and menstrual cramps. Pudina is also used as a natural insect repellent.

**Salt** *(Namak)*: Used in most dishes as well as salads, breads, and drinks.

**Sesame Seeds** *(Dona-e-Kunjid)*: Sprinkled on bread and Rhote. Sesame seeds are very nutritious. They contain a lot of protein and make a great addition to all kinds of dishes such as salads or pastries. Sesame seeds protect the body from free radicals and have been shown to lower cholesterol.

**Rose Water (***Ab-e-Gulab***)**: Used in Halwa, Firnee, Shirbirinj, and other desserts. Commonly used as an aphrodisiac or in skin care products due to their beneficial properties for healthy skin.

**Saffron** *(Zaffron)*: Mostly used in Palau and Chalau along with some desserts. Saffron is a very expensive spice. It is very expensive to produce and it takes 20,000 stigmas to produce one pound of saffron. Only very small quantities are used in dishes and desserts. Saffron is believed to be beneficial for fever and cramps.

**Turmeric** *(Zard Choba)*: Used in many afghan dishes like quarma, palau, and desserts. Turmeric has a strong flavor and should be used in moderation. Turmeric has anti-inflammatory benefits and is a natural antiseptic and antibacterial agent. Turmeric is also good for digestion.

Research has shown that turmeric strengthens the gallbladder, inhibits dangerous blood clotting, reduces liver toxins, and helps the liver metabolize fats. Turmeric is also believed to aid in weight loss.

## ***Other common ingredients used in Afghan dishes***

**Alou Bukhara** (Bukhara Plum): This is the plum usually found in Bukhara. Found mainly in Central Asia but can be bought in Afghan and Iranian grocery stores. Used dry in quarma's like meatball.

**Dal**: A lentil used to make the dish Dal. Dal is easily found in Indian grocery stores as well as Afghan stores. The small orange lentils are called Masoor Dal and the small yellow lentils are called Toor (or Toovar) Dal. I normally like to mix the toor and masoor dal and cook together.

**Eggplant** *(Banjan)*: This can be the regular eggplant or the Japanese size eggplants. Used in quarmas and Banjan Bourani.

**Garbanzo Beans** *(Nakhud)*: Also called chick peas and used in various dishes, including aush, soups, and shour nakhud. Can use canned or dry garbanzo beans.

**Long Grain Rice** *(Birinj-e-Luk)*: This rice is used in dishes like Kitchiree Quroot and Shoula. Although the name implies long grains of rice, it's actually shorter than the basmati rice kernels.

**Kidney Beans** (*Lobiya*): Usually red kidney beans and used in soup and quarmas. Can use canned or dry beans.

**Mung Beans** *(Maush)*: Green split pea type beans used in Kitchiree Quroot and Maushawa.

**Onion** *(Piaz)*: Basic ingredient in most Afghan dishes and used in almost all quarmas, soups, kabobs, Kitchiree Quroot, and Palau. The benefits of onions on our health are numerous, especially for boosting our immune system.

**Potatoes** *(Kachaloo)*: Basic brown Russet potatoes used in soups, quarmas, Kachaloo Bourani, and Boulani.

**Rice** *(Birinj)* (Extra Fancy long grain Rice): This is usually Basmati rice used in Chalau's and Palau's.

**Oleaster** (*Sinjit)*: An import from Afghanistan and normally used as a dry fruit for Mehwa Tar-kada. Also known as Dry Bair.

**Split Peas** *(Dal Nakhud):* Also known as Chana dal. Used in quarmas, soups, and shami kabab. Chana dal is not recommended for making the dish dal.

**Tomatoes** *(Banjan Rumi)*: These are the typical common tomatoes. Used in salads, quarmas, soups, etc.

**Tomato Paste** *(Rhub-e-banjan rumi)*: Very common ingredient in Afghan cooking. Used in almost all quarmas, soups, Palau, Kachaloo Bourani, etc. It has been recommended we consume at least 10 tablespoons of tomato paste a week for optimum health.

# Quroot, Yogurt, Chaka, Doughe & Qaymagh

# Mahst (Yogurt)

*Afghan yogurt or "Mahst" is a regular staple in Afghan cuisine. It has a very rich and refreshing taste. It is served plain or with crushed dry mint. Mahst is served either as a side dish or as a topping on such dishes as Kadu Bourani, Kachaloo Bourani, Banjan Bourani, or Kitchiree Quroot. I make homemade organic yogurt regularly and it comes out better than the store bought variety.*

For your first batch of homemade yogurt, use plain commercial yogurt (preferably one with no preservatives) as your starter. From then on, save at least ½ cup from your last batch as the starter for your next batch. It is important to use clean utensils. Use very fresh whole or 1-2% low fat milk. The temperature of the milk needs to be just right before adding it to the starter. For the most accurate measurement, use a basic food thermometer and make sure the milk is 120° Fahrenheit prior to adding to the starter. If you don't have a thermometer handy, you can use your finger or wrist to determine the temperature. If you stick your finger in the milk or drop some on your wrist and you don't burn but the milk is still fairly warm, the milk is ready to be added to the starter.

Need:
½ gallon milk
½ cup plain yogurt starter
Large glass bowl with lid
Thermometer
Large kitchen towels

1. Place the milk in a saucepan and turn the heat on high. Turn off the heat once the milk begins to bubble and rise.

2. Remove the milk from heat and set aside to cool to 120° F or until the milk feels comfortably warm to your little finger or when dropped on your wrist. Remove any film that has formed on the milk and discard.
3. Put the yogurt starter in the large glass bowl and stir in about ½ cup of the warm milk until the starter is completely dissolved, stirring gently to blend. Add the remainder of the milk to the starter and put the lid on the bowl.
4. Put the covered bowl in a corner of your kitchen. Cover the bowl with clean dry towels. Let stand undisturbed until the yogurt is set, about 8-10 hours.
5. After 8-10 hours, remove the towels and place the bowl in the refrigerator for storage. Usually up to 1-2 weeks.

## Doughe (Yogurt Drink)

*Doughe is a refreshingly cool drink especially during the hot summer days. The combination of salt, cucumber, and dried crushed mint works wonders at quenching your thirst.*

1-2 cups of yogurt
1 pitcher of ice water
Salt (to taste)
A pinch of crushed dried mint
1 cucumber (peeled and finely chopped)

1. Place the yogurt in a pitcher and beat into a paste. Gradually add the water, stirring constantly.
2. Add the salt, mint, and cucumber. Mix well.
3. Serve in glasses.

# *Chaka (Yogurt Spread)*

*Chaka is a wonderful and healthy alternative to sour cream. Chaka can be spread on bread or used as a dip for chips or vegetables.*

4 cups plain yogurt
1-2 teaspoons of salt (or more to taste)
Cheese cloth bag or sheets (10"X10")

1. At least one day before serving, mix the salt into the yogurt.
2. Line a colander with 4 single layers of cheesecloth. Pour the yogurt into the cheesecloth. Gather the corners into a bag and tie them together securely with a cord.
3. Hang the bag over the kitchen faucet high enough to drain into the sink, or suspend over a deep bowl (The chaka can remain in the colander but hanging it allows more drainage resulting in firmer chaka). Allow the chaka to drain overnight or until the yogurt is firm. The texture should be the consistency of softened cream cheese. Remove from the bag and place in a covered container.
4. Refrigerate the chaka overnight.
5. Dip Option: Mix the chaka with crushed dry mint and serve with chips or vegetables.

# Quroot

*Quroot is made from drained, salted, and dried yogurt. Quroot can be used as a substitute to plain yogurt for dishes such as Kitchiree Quroot, Kadu Bourani, Aushak, and Mantu. To prepare Quroot for serving with particular dishes, the ball is soaked in hot water and then liquefied in a blender. Although Quroot can easily be found in Afghan grocery stores, it can easily be made at home.*

### *Homemade Quroot*

1. Put 4 cups of yogurt in a pot and bring to a boil. Allow to boil for 2-3 minutes and remove from stove.
2. Add about ¼ cup of salt.
3. Line a colander with cheese cloth and put the yogurt in the colander. Bag up the cheese cloth and tie a knot. Hang the cheese cloth over the sink and allow to drain.
4. Once drained, take out the yogurt and make small balls out of the drained yogurt. Place balls in a tray and set out for a few days until they become hard.
5. Store the dried balls in a cool dry place. They will last a long time. Use as needed.

# Qaymagh

*Qaymagh is a rich and thick cream usually eaten for breakfast. It is absolutely delicious with sugar and cardamom sprinkled on top and eaten with warm Afghan bread. The Qaymagh can also be added to tea or coffee.*

4 cups of half & half cream
1 cup milk

1. Place ¼ cup of milk and 4 cups of half & half in a deep, high walled skillet.
2. Blend the half & half and milk with an electric mixer until it froths.
3. Turn on the heat and bring the mixture to a boil. Stir the cream constantly so it doesn't boil over or burn.
4. Reduce the heat to medium low and allow the mixture to reduce.
5. As the mixture is reducing, a thin layer will form on top. Remove the top layer with a slotted spoon and put in a bowl. Repeat this process of removing the top layer until all the mixture has thickened and reduced in the pan.
6. Place all thickened cream in a bowl and allow to cool.
7. Add an additional ½ cup of milk over the cream and refrigerate.
8. Serve with warm toasted Afghan bread and sprinkle with sugar and cardamom.

# Sharbat e-Raihan (Basil Drink)

*This drink takes me back to my childhood and I have fond memories about the first time I tasted it. It's a drink usually reserved for special occasions but one I think we should drink on a regular basis due to its health benefits. The basil seeds, after being soaked in water, reportedly help to detoxify our blood, remove impurities from our intestines, remove bloating, and have the same effect of antibiotics in eliminating bacteria from our body. The drink works best if taken at night but is a refreshing treat any time of day.*

1 tablespoon basil seeds
½ teaspoon rosewater
Sugar (to taste)

1. In a glass pitcher, add the basil seeds and fill the pitcher with water. Allow to soak for 1-2 hours.
2. Once a grey coated jelly like cover forms on the seeds, add the sugar and rosewater. Stir. Add more sugar if desired.
3. Serve chilled.

*Basil seeds after being soaked in water*

# Sides: Salad, Chutney, Tourshie, etc.

## ***Salata (Salad)***

*The Afghan salad, "Sa-laa-ta", is a simple combination of fresh tomatoes, onions, and fresh mint chopped into small pieces. Add some salt and mix well. The traditional Afghan salad makes a delicious supplement to the food. Afghan salad is eaten WITH the food not before or after the meal.*

2-3 tomatoes (finely chopped)
1 red onion (finely chopped)
5-10 sprigs of fresh mint (finely chopped)
Salt (to taste)

## Hummus

*Hummus is not a traditional Afghan dish but goes well with Afghan Bread. Hummus is very rich in protein and taste.*

2 cans of garbanzo beans
3-4 big tablespoons of tahini sauce
3-4 cloves of garlic
½ to 1 teaspoon salt
1 lemon (juiced)
1 teaspoon olive oil
Black pepper (to taste)
¼ cup of water

1. Rinse and drain the garbanzo beans and place in a food processor.
2. Add the tahini sauce, garlic, salt, oil, lemon juice, water, and pepper. Blend until smooth.
3. Add additional water, salt, and lemon juice as needed.
4. Serve with toasted pita bread or traditional Afghan bread.

## Baba Ganoush

*Although baba ganoush is not a traditional Afghan dish, we have a similar dish called Burta. Baba ganoush tastes delicious with Afghan Bread.*

2 eggplants
4-5 cloves of garlic (sliced)
2-3 tablespoons tahini sauce
½ teaspoon salt
1 lemon (juiced)
1 teaspoon olive oil
Black pepper (to taste)
¼ cup of water (as needed).

1. Wash and cut eggplants in half.
2. Stud the eggplant halves with slices of garlic (stick garlic inside the eggplant meat and skin).
3. Bake or broil the eggplant for 10-15 minutes.
4. Once the eggplant is soft, take out of the oven and allow to cool.
5. Spoon out the meat of the eggplant and discard the skin.
6. In a food processor, add the eggplant, salt, lemon juice, oil, pepper, tahini sauce, and water. Blend well.
7. Add more lemon and salt as needed.
8. Serve with toasted pita or afghan bread.

## Shour Nakhud

*This side dish is perfect for picnics or outdoor BBQ's. The combination of beans, cilantro chutney and vinegar is delicious and refreshing.*

2 cans of garbanzo beans
1 can of kidney beans
1 cup of cilantro chutney (recipe below)
4-5 potatoes
Salt
Pepper
Crushed chili peppers
1 cup of apple cider vinegar

1. Wash the potatoes with the skin and put in a deep-dish pot.
2. Add a little bit of salt along with 5-6 cups of water and boil until the potatoes are soft.
3. Drain the water and allow the potatoes to cool.
4. Once the potatoes are cool, peel the skin from the potatoes and slice them from the top down in a big bowl. They should be thin, circular slices of potato.

5. Rinse the garbanzo beans and kidney beans prior to adding to the potatoes.
6. Add the cilantro chutney, salt, pepper, and chili peppers along with the vinegar and mix.
7. Allow to chill in the refrigerator prior to serving.

## *Chutney Gashneez (Cilantro Chutney)*

1-2 bunches of fresh cilantro (thoroughly washed)
2-3 cloves of garlic
1-2 serrano chili peppers
1 cup of apple cider vinegar
Salt to taste
¼ cup of walnuts (optional)

1. In a blender, blend the cilantro, garlic, peppers, and walnuts with ½ cup of vinegar.
2. Add more vinegar as needed to give it a liquid consistency. Add salt. Blend and taste.
3. Add more garlic, vinegar, or peppers as needed to make it the desired spice level.
4. Store in the refrigerator.

## *Chutney Murch-e-Surkh (Red Pepper)*

4 large red bell peppers
6 small red chili peppers (Skinny peppers)
1 cup apple cider vinegar
One whole garlic bulb (minced)
6 oz. of tomato paste
1 teaspoon of sia dana (black caraway seeds)
Salt to taste
1 tablespoon of sugar

1. Wash the bell peppers and take out the seeds.
2. Put in a blender along with vinegar.
3. Blend until pureed.
4. Put in a pot and boil for 5-10 minutes.
5. Liquefy the tomato paste with a little bit of water and then add to the pot.
6. Boil for 30-40 minutes and let cool.
7. Add the minced garlic, sugar, salt and sia dana to the pot and mix together.
8. Place the hot mixture in jars and seal the jars.
9. Store in a cool dry place.

## Tourshie Banjan (Pickled Eggplant)

*This tourshie is a specialty of my aunt Magul so I'm grateful that she shared her recipe with me. The following recipes are very different than the commercial pickled vegetables you get at the stores. I have not tasted commercial pickled vegetables as good as these, ever. I think the mint and sia dana make the taste unique.*

3 lbs. Japanese Eggplant
1 bulb of garlic
1 lb. carrots
1-2 tablespoons dried crushed red pepper
1 lb. mix of fresh red and green jalapeno peppers (the fat long peppers)
1 teaspoon salt
2-3 tablespoon sia dana (black caraway seeds)
2-3 tablespoon dried crushed mint
4-5 cups apple cider vinegar

1. Select soft small Japanese eggplant.
2. Wash the eggplant and clip the green leaves by the stem.
3. Split the eggplant from the bottom to the stem (lengthwise) but do not cut all the way through. Stop right before the stem.

4. In a cooking pot, fill ¾ way with water and boil the eggplant for 5-10 minutes until tender but not too soft. Drain the eggplant in a colander and allow to cool for a few hours (4-5 hours or overnight).
5. In a bowl mix the sia dana, mint, salt, and crushed red pepper (spice mix).
6. Slice the garlic cloves thinly (use entire bulb).
7. In a jar big enough to hold all the ingredients, layer a few of the eggplants in a circle and then add a few jalapeno peppers over the eggplant. Sprinkle with the spice mix and garlic. Continue this process alternating eggplant, peppers, and spice mix until all are in the jar.
8. Add vinegar in the jar and fill the jar to about 1 inch above vegetable level.
9. Seal the jar tight and allow to sit for 3-4 days.
10. After 3-4 days, it's ready to be served with your favorite dish such as Chalau and Quarma.

## ***Tourshie Tarkari (Pickled Mixed Vegetables)***

1 lb. Carrots
1 lb. Cauliflower tips
1 lb. Japanese Eggplant
½ lb. Turnips
1 lb. mix of fresh red and green jalapeno peppers (the fat peppers)
1 bulb of garlic
1-2 tablespoons dried crushed red pepper
1 teaspoon salt
2-3 tablespoon sia dana (black caraway seeds)
2-3 tablespoon dried crushed mint
4-5 cups Apple cider vinegar

1. Wash and peel carrots. Cut into quarters.
2. Wash and peel turnips. Cut into quarters.
3. Wash the eggplant and clip the green leaves by the stem.

4. Split the eggplant from the bottom to the stem (lengthwise) but do not cut all the way through. Stop right before the stem.
5. Wash Cauliflower tips gently.
6. Fill a big pot ¾ of the way with water and add carrots and turnips. Boil for about 5-10 minutes or until cooked.
7. Add the eggplant and cook for an additional 5 minutes.
8. Add the cauliflower tips and boil for an additional 2 minutes.
9. Drain all the vegetables gently in a colander. Allow to cool for 1-2 hours. (The vegetables must be completely cooled prior to being pickled in order to avoid mildew forming on them).
10. In a bowl mix the sia dana, mint, salt, and crushed red pepper (spice mix).
11. Slice the garlic cloves thinly (use entire bulb).
12. In a jar big enough to hold all the ingredients, layer a few carrots in a circle, add turnips, eggplant, and cauliflower tips, and then add a few jalapeno peppers over the vegetables. Sprinkle with spice mix and garlic. Continue this process alternating vegetables, peppers, and spice mix until all are in the jar.
13. Add the vinegar in the jar and fill jar to about 1 inch above vegetable level.
14. Seal jar tight and allow to sit for 3-4 days.
15. After 3-4 days, it's ready to be served with your favorite dinner dish such as Chalau and Quarma.

*Tourshie Tarkari*

# Appetizers

## Bouranis

(Kachaloo, Banjan, & Kadu)

## Boulani & Dal

# ***Kachaloo Bourani (Potatoes)***

*This dish is sentimental for me because it was the only Afghan dish I knew to cook when I was living away from home.*

4-5 potatoes
2-3 tablespoons of oil
1-2 tablespoons of tomato puree
3 cloves of garlic (minced)
1teaspoon of turmeric
1-2 tablespoons coriander
1 teaspoon ginger (fresh grated or ground)
1 cup of yogurt
1 cup of water
1 fresh jalapeno pepper
Salt
Pepper
Crushed dried mint

1. Peel and slice the potatoes thinly (¼ inch).
2. In a frying pan, heat the oil.
3. Turn down the heat to medium and add 2 cloves of minced garlic to the heated oil. Stir for 1-2 minutes.
4. Add the sliced potatoes and stir for 1-2 minutes.
5. Add the tomato puree, turmeric, coriander, ginger, salt, pepper, and whole jalapeno pepper along with 1 cup of water.
6. Cover the pan with a lid and cook for 8-10 minutes on medium heat until the potatoes are cooked.
7. In a separate bowel add 1 cup of yogurt and 1 clove of minced garlic and mix.
8. Smear some yogurt on a platter and place the potato bourani on the yogurt mixture. Top the potatoes with an additional 2-3 tablespoons of the yogurt mixture and sprinkle with crushed dry mint.
9. Serve with warm toasted Afghan bread.

*Kachaloo Bourani*

## ***Banjan Bourani (Eggplant Dish with Yogurt Sauce)***

*This is also one of my favorite dishes. Although it takes time to make, it's well worth it. You can fry all the eggplants in advance and freeze for later use.*

3 medium size eggplants
Oil for frying
½ cup of water
3-4 cloves of minced garlic
1 teaspoon ginger (fresh grated or ground)
2 tomatoes (sliced)
1 teaspoon turmeric
1-2 jalapeno peppers
1 cup of plain yogurt
Crushed dried mint
Salt

1. Wash the eggplant and cut from top to bottom in rings ½ inch thick and place the eggplant in a large colander.

2. Slash (3 times) the center of the eggplant rings with a knife and sprinkle with salt. Sprinkle the salt liberally on the eggplant rings and allow the eggplant to sit for 3-4 hours. This allows the water to drain from the eggplant.
3. After 3 hours, dry the eggplant with a paper towel.
4. In a deep-dish skillet, heat 1 ½ -2 cups of oil and lightly fry the eggplant until browned on both sides. Remove the eggplant from the skillet and set aside.
5. Drain the oil out of the skillet and put the eggplant back in the skillet.
6. Add the garlic, ginger, a pinch of salt, and 1 teaspoon of turmeric along with ½ cup of water.
7. Place the sliced tomatoes over the eggplant and add the whole jalapeno peppers.
8. Cover the skillet with a lid and cook on medium heat for 10-15 minutes.
9. In a bowl, mix 1 cup of yogurt with 1 clove of minced garlic.
10. In a platter, smear 1-2 tablespoons of yogurt mixture on the bottom.
11. Gently remove the eggplant and tomatoes and place on the yogurt.
12. Spoon out 3-4 tablespoons of the yogurt mix over the entire eggplant.
13. Sprinkle crushed dried mint over the yogurt and eggplant.
14. Serve with warm toasted Afghan bread and additional yogurt if desired.

*Banjan Bourani*

## ***Kadu Bourani (Pumpkin Dish with Yogurt Sauce)***

*Kadu Bourani is always a hit with Westerner's at Afghan restaurants. The sugar pie pumpkin makes the best kadu bourani.*

1 medium sized pumpkin (cut into thin slices)
1 small onion (diced)
1-2 tablespoon coriander
1 teaspoon turmeric
Salt
3-4 cloves of minced garlic
1 tablespoon sugar
¼ - ½ cup of oil
1-2 jalapeno pepper
1 cup of water
1 cup of yogurt
Crushed dried mint

1. In a deep set skillet heat the oil on high heat.

2. Reduce the heat to medium and sauté the pumpkin slices until lightly browned.
3. Remove the pumpkin from the skillet and set aside.
4. Add the onions to the skillet and sauté the onions until light golden brown.
5. Add the pumpkin back to the skillet along with the coriander, turmeric, salt, 1-2 cloves of minced garlic, sugar, and pepper, and top with ½- ¾ cup of water.
6. Cover the skillet and cook on low for about 10-15 minutes.
7. In a cup, mix the yogurt with 1-2 cloves of minced garlic.
8. In a platter, smear 1-2 tablespoons of yogurt mixture on the bottom.
9. Gently remove the pumpkin and place on the yogurt.
10. Spoon out 3-4 tablespoons of the yogurt mix over the entire pumpkin.
11. Sprinkle crushed dried mint over the yogurt and pumpkin.
12. Serve with warm toasted Afghan bread and additional yogurt if desired.

## ***Boulani Kachaloo (Potatoes)***

*Boulani is probably the most popular dish at Afghan restaurants. It tastes great with yogurt and cilantro chutney.*

4-5 green leeks or Gundana (washed thoroughly and chopped)
1 onion (sliced)
5-6 potatoes (boiled and peeled)
1 teaspoon crushed red peppers
Salt (to taste)
1 teaspoon black pepper
Dough mix (use recipe for Aushak) or Chinese pasta wraps (large square)
Oil for frying

1. Either follow the dough mix recipe or use Chinese pasta wraps.
2. Optional: Sauté the onions to light golden brown and set aside.
3. Mash the boiled potatoes either with your hand, a potato masher, or put through the meat grinder to mix.
4. Take the potato mix and add the gundana (or leeks), onions (optional), salt, black pepper, and crushed red peppers. Knead the mix well. Check the salt level and add more as needed.
5. If using dough, take out a small piece of dough and make into a ball. Then flatten the ball with a rolling pin, sprinkling with flour to prevent sticking. Make the ball very thin and round.
6. Using either the dough or the pasta wraps, take a small amount of the potato mix and place in the middle of the wraps.
7. Dip your fingers in water and wet the edges of the wrap.
8. Fold the wrap over and press the edges. Sprinkle flour on top to prevent sticking. Cover to prevent from drying out and set aside. Follow this process for the remainder of the potato mixture.
9. Once all the wraps have been filled, heat ½ cup of oil in a deep set skillet. Once the oil is hot, turn the heat down to medium low.
10. Place 2-3 filled wraps in the skillet and brown slowly on both sides. Press the wraps with a spatula to remove the air pockets.
11. Once golden brown, remove the wraps from oil, allowing oil to drip back into skillet for a few seconds prior to placing it on the platter. Put a paper towel on the platter to catch the oil. Continue this process until all the wraps have been fried. Add oil to the skillet as needed.
12. Serve hot with yogurt and cilantro chutney.

# Dal

*Dal is traditionally an Indo/Pakistani dish but has become a favorite among Afghans. The Afghan version of dal that I'm familiar with is very different from the traditional Indian version. Dal in general is a very easy and nutritious meal full of protein. It can be a side dish to Chalau or a meal on its own.*

1 cup of Dal (washed and soaked in advance)
½ onion (chopped)
4-5 tablespoons of oil
2-3 cups of water
1-2 tablespoons coriander
1 teaspoon of turmeric
1 teaspoon of salt
1-2 teaspoon ginger (fresh grated or ground)
2-3 large tomatoes
½ teaspoon ground red chili pepper
½ cup chopped cilantro
2-3 cloves of garlic (minced)

1. In a sauce pan, sauté the onion in oil until slightly browned.
2. Add the water, dal, turmeric, coriander, ginger, salt, chili pepper, and cilantro.
3. Cover the pot with a lid and cook for about 15-20 minutes on medium heat.
4. While the dal is cooking, bring some water to a boil and pour over the tomatoes.
5. Peel the tomatoes and chop them in quarters.
6. In a skillet, heat 1-2 tablespoons of oil and add 2 gloves of minced garlic. Sauté the garlic until light brown.
7. Add the tomatoes and sprinkle some salt.
8. Cover the pot and cook on low for 10-15 minutes.

9. When the tomatoes have cooked, mash them with a spatula until it becomes a sauce. Simmer the sauce on low heat for another 10 minutes.
10. When the dal has thickened, remove the dal from the pot and put in a bowl.
11. Add the tomato mixture on top but don't mix.
12. Serve with Chalau or warm toasted Afghan bread.

*Dal*

Tohkum
(Eggs)

*All the egg dishes taste great with green chutney and afghan bread. These dishes are usually eaten for lunch or dinner but they make great breakfast dishes as well.*

## ***Tokhum Kachaloo (Eggs with Potatoes Omelet)***

4 eggs
2-3 tablespoons oil
1 bell pepper (chopped)
1 onion
1 potato
1 tomato
Salt (to taste)
Pepper (to taste)
Red crushed pepper

1. Slice the onion.
2. In a skillet, heat the oil and sauté the onion until transparent on medium low heat.
3. Peel and cut the potato in small pieces.
4. Add the potatoes to the onions and stir together. Cover the skillet with a lid and allow to cook on medium low heat until the potatoes become tender.
5. In a bowl mix the eggs with salt, pepper, and red crushed pepper.
6. Stir in the egg and mix with the onion and potatoes.
7. Chop the tomato and bell pepper and add to the eggs. Stir and mix with the eggs.
8. Cook until eggs and vegetables are cooked.
9. Serve with bread and green chutney.

## ***Tokhum Gundana (Eggs with Leeks Omelet)***

½ cup chopped gundana (or leeks)
4 eggs
2-3 tablespoons of oil
Salt (to taste)
Pepper (to taste)

1. Wash the gundana thoroughly and cut in small pieces.
2. Heat the oil in a frying pan and stir the gundana for 2-3 minutes on medium low heat.
3. In a separate bowl, mix the eggs with salt and pepper.
4. Add the eggs to the gundana and mix together.
5. Cook until the eggs are ready.
6. Serve with bread.

# ***Tokhum Khageena (Egg Omelet)***

4 eggs
1 onion
1 jalapeno pepper
½ cup of cilantro
2-3 tablespoons of oil
½ cup all purpose flour
Salt (to taste)
Pepper (to taste)

1. Dice onions, jalapeno pepper, and cilantro.
2. In a separate bowl beat eggs well.
3. Add the flour, onions, jalapeno peppers, salt, pepper, and cilantro to the eggs and mix.
4. In a frying pan, heat oil and add the egg mixture.
5. Brown one side and flip to brown other side.
6. Serve with bread.

## ***Tokhum Banjan Rumi (Eggs with Tomato Omelet)***

4 eggs
4 tomatoes
2-3 tablespoons of oil
1 medium onion
1 jalapeno pepper (diced)
¼ cup of cilantro (chopped)
¼ cup of mushroom (chopped)-optional
¼ cup of potatoes (chopped)-optional
Salt (to taste)
Pepper (to taste)

1. In a frying pan, heat the oil.
2. Dice the onion and tomatoes.
3. Sauté the onions in the oil until golden brown.
4. Optional: add the potatoes with the onions in a covered skillet until tender.
5. Optional: add the mushrooms to the potatoes for 3-4 minutes on medium low heat.
6. In a separate bowl mix the eggs and tomatoes along with the jalapeno peppers and cilantro.
7. Add the egg mixture to the skillet and sprinkle with salt and pepper.
8. Stir the eggs and vegetable mix until the eggs are cooked.
9. Serve with bread and cilantro chutney.

## ***Kachaloo & Banjan Rumi Tokhum (Eggs with Potatoes and Tomatoes)***

3-4 eggs
2-3 tablespoons oil
1 onion (sliced)
2-3 small potatoes
2-3 tomatoes
Salt (to taste)
Pepper (to taste)

1. In a skillet, heat the oil and sauté the onions until transparent on medium low heat (3-5 minutes).
2. Peel and cut the potatoes in small pieces.
3. Add the potatoes to the onions and stir together. Cover the skillet with a lid and allow to cook on medium low heat for 5-7 minutes.
4. Add the tomatoes, stir in the salt and pepper, and cover the skillet to cook for an additional 5 minutes.
5. Crack the eggs and drop the eggs on the tomato/potato mixture in the skillet.
6. Cover the skillet and allow to cook until the egg yolks become thick and have a white covering.
7. Serve with bread and green chutney.

Rice
Dishes

# Chalau (Steamed Basmati Rice)

*Chalau is one of the main dishes in Afghan cooking. It is very versatile and can be served with the quarmas and/or fish dishes.*

2 cups of white basmati rice
2-3 tablespoons of vegetable oil
Salt
6-8 cups of water for rice to cook in
1 clean kitchen cloth big enough to cover the lid

1. Wash the rice thoroughly until the water runs clear, drain and add fresh water to cover rice.
2. Add salt (1-2 tablespoons) and let soak for at least 30 minutes to several hours.
3. In a deep-dish pot, fill midway with water.
4. Add 2-3 tablespoons of salt and bring to a boil.
5. Take ¾ cup of water from the pot and set aside.
6. Drain the rice and add to the boiling water.
7. Stir the rice until it comes to a boil.
8. Check the grains for softness on the outside but the core should be a little hard. If it overcooks, it becomes sticky and mushy. It should not boil for more than 5 minutes.
9. Once the right consistency is reached, drain the rice in a colander and put back into pot.
10. Add the cup of reserved water to the rice.
11. Add oil.
12. Mix and bring to a mound.
13. Put several holes in the mound with the end of the spoon.
14. Put the lid in the cloth and wrap the lid in the cloth. Overlap the cloth corners over the lid. Place the lid on the pot (see picture illustration).
15. Turn the heat on high until steam comes out from under the lid.

16. After steam comes out from under the lid, turn the heat to low and cook for about 20 minutes.
17. Take out the rice and serve with any quarma.

*Note: This dish becomes easier with practice. To reheat left-over chalau, add ¼ cup of water and heat the rice on medium low heat in a covered pot.

Step 1: Put lid on large towel

Step 2: Wrap towel over lid

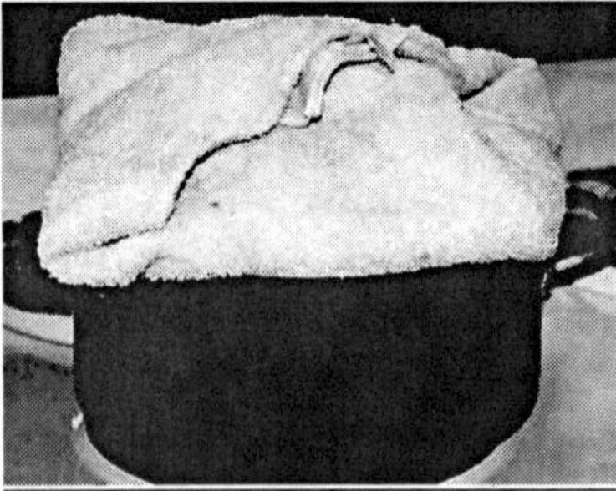

Step 3: Cover rice with wrapped lid

## Qabli Palau (Rice with chicken, raisins, and carrots)

*Palau is a very popular and favorite Afghan dish. There are many variations of Palau including but not limited to: Sabzi Palau (Spinach), Yakhnee Palau (with lamb in steamed rice), and Narinj Palau (orange peel and rice). I only included the Chicken Qabli Palau and Maush Palau here.*

*Qabli Palau is probably the most popular dish at formal and informal dinner parties. Some make this dish with beef or lamb but in our house, we usually make it with chicken.*

2 breasts of chicken (cut in quarters)
1 medium onion (sliced)
3 cups of basmati rice
½ cup of oil
2 tablespoons of tomato paste
2 teaspoons cinnamon
1 teaspoon of cumin
1 teaspoon of ground cloves
1 teaspoon of ground cardamom
1 teaspoon salt
2 carrots (julienned)
½ cup of black raisins
Water

1. Wash the rice thoroughly and then soak in water. Sprinkle 2 tablespoons of salt and allow to soak for 1-2 hours.
2. Spice Mix: In a container, mix the cinnamon, cumin, cloves, and cardamom. Set aside.
3. Heat the oil in a deep-dish pot and caramelize the onions (brown and slightly crispy).

4. Drain the oil out of the pot in a separate bowl then finely grind the onions to a pulp in the pot with a wooden spoon.
5. Add the oil back in the pot, along with the tomato paste, and 2-3 cups of water. Boil for 3-4 minutes.
6. Wash the chicken and remove the excess fat.
7. Add the chicken to the onions along with 1 tablespoon of the spice mix and a ¼ tsp. of salt. Allow to cook for 15 minutes.
8. Remove the chicken from the pot and set aside.
9. Strain the liquid from the mixture in a bowl using a mesh strainer. The leftovers in the strainer can be discarded. Keep the liquid and set aside.
10. Wash the raisins and set aside.
11. In a small frying pan, add a small amount of oil and lightly sauté the carrots for 1-2 minutes. Remove and set aside.
12. In a separate pot, add 6-8 cups of water. Add salt to the water and bring to a boil. Drain the water from the rice and add to the boiling water. Allow to boil for 3-4 minutes. Check the rice by tasting one kernel and test whether it's al dente. Rice should be soft on the outside and slightly hard on the inside.
13. Drain the rice in a colander.
14. Place the drained rice back in the pot. Add ¾ -1 cup of onion liquid over the rice and mix. Add ½ teaspoon of spice mix over the rice and mix in with the rice. Add more salt as needed.
15. Place the chicken in the center of the rice. Pull the rice over the chicken and form a mound. Put several holes in the mound with the end of the spoon.
16. Add carrots and raisins over the mound. Use a clean cloth to wrap the lid in and cover the pot. Cook on medium low heat for 30-40 minutes.
17. After 30-40 minutes, take out ¾ of the rice and put in a big platter. Separate the chicken, carrots, and raisins. Set aside.

18. Put the chicken on the rice and cover with the remaining ¼ of rice. Top the rice with carrots and raisins and serve (see picture illustration).

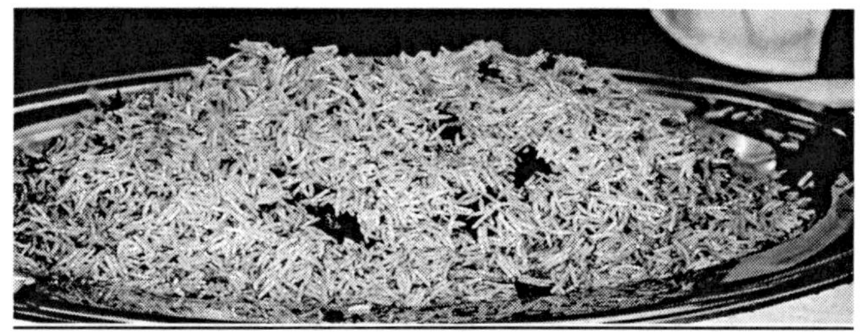

# Maush Palau

*This dish can be made with beef or lamb as well as without any meat at all. For the vegetarian version, follow the steps for the onion liquid base but omit the chicken from the ingredients. You can eat this plain or serve with a side dish of bourani banjan or kadu, salad, or quarma.*

2 ½ cups of basmati rice
1 cup mung beans
2 breasts of chicken (cut in quarters)
1 medium onion (sliced)
½ cup of oil
2 tablespoons of tomato paste
2 teaspoons cinnamon
1 teaspoon of cumin
1 teaspoon of ground cloves
1 teaspoon of ground cardamom
1 teaspoon salt
Water

1. Wash the rice thoroughly and then soak in water. Sprinkle 2 tablespoons of salt and allow to soak for 1-2 hours.
2. Wash the mung beans and soak in water.
3. Spice Mix: In a container, mix the cinnamon, cumin, cloves, and cardamom. Set aside.
4. Heat the oil in a deep-dish pot and caramelize the onions (brown and slightly crispy).
5. Drain the oil out of the pot in a separate bowl then finely grind the onions to a pulp in the pot with a wooden spoon.
6. Add the oil back in the pot, along with the tomato paste, and 2-3 cups of water. Boil for 3-4 minutes.
7. Wash the chicken and remove the excess fat.

8. Add the chicken to the onions along with 1 tablespoon of the spice mix and a ¼ tsp. of salt. Allow to cook for 15 minutes.
9. Remove the chicken from the pot and set aside.
10. Strain the liquid from the mixture in a bowl using a mesh strainer. The leftovers in the strainer can be discarded. Keep the liquid and set aside.
11. In a separate pot, add 6-8 cups of water. Add salt to the water and bring to a boil. Drain the water from the rice and add to the boiling water. Allow to boil for 3-4 minutes. Check the rice by tasting one kernel and test whether it's al dente. Rice should be soft on the outside and slightly hard on the inside.
12. At the same time, in an additional separate pot, bring water to a boil and add the drained mung beans. Boil on medium high heat for 5 minutes.
13. Drain the rice in a colander.
14. Drain the cooked mung beans on top of the rice.
15. Place the drained rice and mung bean mix back in the pot. Add ½ -¾ cup of onion liquid over the rice and mix. Add ½ teaspoon of spice mix over the rice and mix in with the rice. Add more salt as needed.
16. Place the chicken in the center of the rice. Pull the rice over the chicken and form a mound. Put several holes in the mound with the end of the spoon.
17. Use a clean cloth to wrap the lid in and cover the pot. Cook on medium low heat for 20-30 minutes.
18. When ready, take ¾ of the rice out and put on a platter. Separate the chicken and set aside. Put the chicken on the rice and cover with the remaining ¼ of rice.
19. Serve.

*Maush Palau*

## ***Kitchiree Quroot***

*This is one of my favorite dishes since I was a child. This dish can be vegetarian or served with the basic ground beef sauce.*

2-3 tablespoons of oil
2 cups birinj luk (long grain rice)
¼ onion (sliced)
½ cup mung beans
7-8 cups of water
½ teaspoon of fresh or ground ginger
1-2 teaspoons of salt
¼ teaspoon of black pepper
½ teaspoon coriander
1 cup plain yogurt or quroot
1-2 cloves of minced garlic
3 tablespoons of oil
1 whole jalapeno pepper
Crushed dry mint (optional)

1. Wash the rice thoroughly, and allow to soak in clean water for 2-3 hours.
2. Wash the mung beans thoroughly and allow to soak for 2-3 hours.
3. In a pressure cooker, heat the oil and caramelize the onions.
4. Add the mung beans and stir with the onions for 1-2 minutes.
5. Drain the water from the soaked rice and put in the pressure cooker along with 4-5 cups of water, coriander, salt, pepper, jalapeno pepper, and ginger. Cook in the pressure cooker for 10-15 minutes. Check to see if cooked (ingredients soft).
6. In a frying pan, heat the garlic in oil for 1-2 minutes until lightly browned.
7. In a separate bowl (make sure the bottom is clean), place the yogurt.
8. Pour the oil and garlic mixture over the yogurt.
9. Mix the kitchiree rice well in the pressure cooker prior to serving.
10. Place the kitchiree in a platter and make a mound.
11. Insert the bowl of yogurt and garlic mixture over the rice mound, sprinkle mint over the rice (optional).
12. Serve plain or with ground meat sauce.

Alternative to pressure cooker:

- In a deep 5-quart pot, heat the oil and caramelize the onions.
- Add 2-3 cups of water along with the mung beans. Cover the pot and cook for 10 minutes.
- Drain the water from the rice and add the rice to the mung beans along with an additional 2-3 cups of water, coriander, salt, pepper, jalapeno pepper, and ginger. Mix in well and cook in a covered pot on low heat for about 40-45 minutes. Add more water as needed until the rice is cooked.
- Follow steps 6-10 from above.

*Kitchiree Quroot*

## **Dumpokht (rice cooked with chicken and vegetables)**

*This dish is great as a quick and nutritious meal. I usually make this for my daughter. You can make it with or without meat.*

2 cups of basmati rice
¼ cup of oil
1-2 potatoes
½ lb. of chicken breasts
½ onion (sliced)
1 cup frozen vegetable mix of choice
2 tablespoons of tomato paste
2-3 tablespoons coriander
1 teaspoon turmeric
½ teaspoon ground ginger
2 cloves of garlic (minced)
Salt
Pepper
3-4 cups of water

1. Wash the rice thoroughly, and allow to soak in clean water for 2-3 hours.
2. Peel and cut the potatoes in small chunks and set aside.
3. In a medium size saucepan, heat the oil on medium high heat and caramelize the onions until golden brown.
4. Wash the chicken breasts, cut up in small cubes, and sauté with the onions for 2-3 minutes.
5. Add the potatoes to the pan along with 3-4 cups of water. Cover the saucepan and allow to cook for 5-7 minutes on medium high heat.
6. Add the garlic, turmeric, coriander, ginger, salt, pepper, and tomato paste. Mix well.
7. Drain the water from the soaked rice and add to the saucepan. Mix the ingredient together. Add an additional cup of water as needed.
8. Lower the heat, cover the saucepan, and allow to cook for 15-20 minutes or until the ingredients are cooked and water has reduced.
9. Mix the rice and vegetables together prior to serving.

## Shoula

*I love shoula as a comfort food. It is delicious and very easy to make. It especially hits the spot for me on cold rainy days. You can add any ingredients you want to the shoula but I've included the recipe for plain shoula here. On occasion I put frozen vegetables or potatoes in as well for variety.*

2 cups birinj-e-luk
¼ cup of oil
½ onion (sliced)
2 tablespoons of tomato paste
2-3 tablespoons coriander
1 teaspoon turmeric
½ teaspoon ground ginger

2 cloves of garlic (minced)
Salt
Pepper
4-5 cups of water

1. Wash the rice thoroughly, and allow to soak in clean water for 2-3 hours.
2. In a pressure cooker or medium sized pot, heat the oil and caramelize the onions to golden brown.
3. Add 4-5 cups of water along with garlic, turmeric, coriander, ginger, salt, pepper, and tomato paste. Mix well.
4. Drain the water from the soaked rice and add to the pot. Mix the ingredient together.
5. If using a pressure cooker, close the lid and pressure cook for 5-10 minutes. (If using a regular pot, cover the pot, lower the heat to medium and allow to cook for 20-25 minutes. Add more water as needed to cook the rice). *Rice can burn easily so make sure you are paying attention to when the hissing begins and cook no longer than 10 minutes after that.
6. Mix the ingredients well prior to serving. {If the rice is cooked but there is some water standing on the rice, simply stir the water into the rice and serve}.

*Shoula*

## Brown Rice Shoula

*This shoula can made with brown basmati rice or plain brown rice. I use a pressure cooker to speed up the cooking process. You can put any vegetables you desire such as carrots, peas, broccoli, kidney beans, garbanzo beans, etc. I use a frozen vegetable mix that has all of those vegetables in it but fresh vegetables are another option. The dish is great for adults and children. For babies, you can puree the shoula further prior to feeding.*

2 cups brown rice
1 onion (sliced)
3-4 tablespoons of oil
1-2 potatoes (peeled and chopped in small chunks)
1-2 cups frozen vegetable mix
1 chicken breast (optional)
2-3 cloves of garlic (minced)
2-3 tablespoons coriander
1 teaspoon turmeric
¼ teaspoon cumin
¼ teaspoon dill (optional)
1 teaspoon ground ginger

1-2 tablespoons tomato paste (optional)
Salt
Pepper
Water

1. In a pressure cooker, heat the oil and caramelize the onions to golden brown.
2. Wash and cut the chicken breasts in small chunks (optional).
3. Add the chicken to the rice and stir until the chicken becomes white (optional).
4. Add the potatoes, frozen vegetable mix, garlic, coriander, ginger, turmeric, salt, pepper, dill, cumin, tomato paste.
5. Add the rice and mix all the ingredients together.
6. Add 2-3 cups of water (water should be 2-3 inches above the rice mixture).
7. Fasten the pressure cooker lid and allow to cook on high heat for about 15 minutes (7-10 minutes total after the pressure cooker begins to "hiss").
8. Allow the pressure to release prior to opening the lid.
9. Mix the ingredients together and serve.

*Rice can burn easily so make sure you are paying attention to when the hissing begins and cook no longer than 10 minutes after that.

*If not using a pressure cooker, cook the rice in a covered pot for about 20-30 minutes prior to adding the vegetables and spices. Cover the pot and allow to cook for an additional 10-15 minutes on medium low heat.*

Quarma
(Sauces)

*The idea of a quarma appears quite foreign to Westerners, but it's the basic staple of the Afghan meal. At my house, we eat different quarmas with rice on a daily basis. You put the quarma over your rice and eat. The Afghan way to use utensils is to use a spoon to eat with and use the fork to push the food into the spoon; therefore you use both your hands. This method makes eating rice with quarma a lot easier than using just a fork. For vegetarian quarmas, please refer to the vegetarian section of this book.*

## Meat Yakhnee (Meat Sauce Base)

*This is the base for most of the meat based quarma recipes. You can follow the recipes for the quarma dishes that require this as the base and add ingredients as required. My mom prepares this base in large batches and stores it in the freezer. The yakhnee can be stored in ready to use amounts (in 2-3 cup containers). Having the yakhnee prepared in advance saves time and makes preparing a meal easier.*

1 ½ lb. of meat (beef or lamb)
½ cup oil
1 large onion, finely sliced
2 to 3 cloves of garlic (minced)
Water
Salt (to taste)
Freshly ground black pepper (to taste)

1. Cut the meat into ¾ inch cubes.
2. Heat the oil in a heavy pan and caramelize the onions until they are golden brown.
3. Decrease the heat to medium high and add the garlic and meat cubes. Sauté, stirring often, until the meat juices evaporate and the meat begins to brown.

4. Add 2 cups of water along with the salt and black pepper (to taste). Bring to a slow simmer and reduce the heat to medium low.
5. Cover the pan and simmer for 30-45 minutes or until the meat is tender. The amount of time depends on the cut of the meat used.
6. Allow to cool prior to storing in freezer.

## *Quarma Gousht (Beef or Lamb)*

2-3 cups meat yakhnee
½ onion (sliced)
2-3 tablespoons of oil
1-2 jalapeno peppers
1 teaspoon of turmeric
2-3 tablespoons of tomato paste
2-3 cloves of garlic (minced)
1 teaspoon of ginger (fresh grated or ground)
1-2 tablespoon coriander
½ -1 cup of water

1. Prepare the meat yakhnee and set aside.
2. In a separate pot, slice the onion and caramelize in oil until light golden brown.
3. Add the meat yakhnee along with the tomato paste, garlic, turmeric, coriander, whole jalapeno peppers, and ginger.
4. Add ½ cup of water if needed and bring to a boil.
5. Reduce the heat and allow to cook in a covered pot for 15-20 minutes.
6. Optional: At this point, you can add your choice of vegetables such as potatoes, cauliflower, carrots, green beans, okra, turnips, or eggplants (wash vegetables and cut in small to medium chunks and add to the quarma) and cover the pot and cook on medium low heat for 10 more minutes.

7. Allow to cook until the liquid has reduced and the oil has surfaced to the top. The sauce should've thickened at this point.
8. Serve with Chalau.

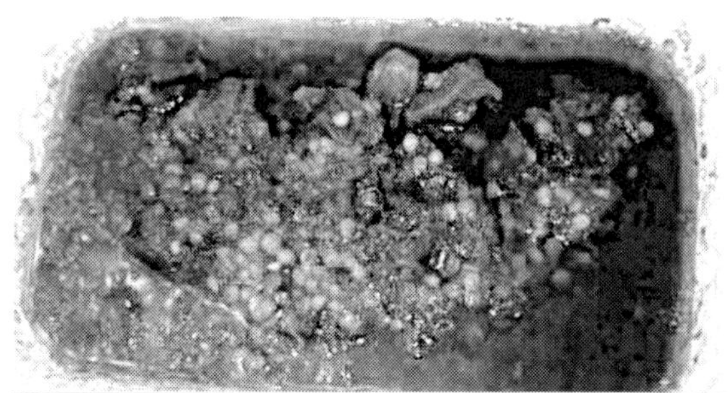

*Quarma Gousht*

## *Kachaloo Quarma (Potato with Beef)*

2-3 cups meat yakhnee
½ onion (sliced)
2-3 tablespoons of oil
3 medium potatoes
1-2 jalapeno peppers
1 teaspoon of turmeric
2-3 cloves of garlic (minced)
2-3 tablespoons of tomato paste
1 teaspoon ginger (fresh grated or ground)
Salt (to taste)
Black pepper (to taste)
½ cup of washed and chopped cilantro
1-2 tablespoon coriander
½-1 cup of water

1. Prepare the meat yakhnee and set aside.
2. In a separate pot, slice the onion and caramelize in oil until light golden brown.

3. Add the meat yakhnee along with the turmeric, coriander, garlic, ginger, salt, pepper, and jalapeno peppers.
4. Add ½ cup of water and bring to a boil.
5. Peel the potatoes and cut in medium sized chunks.
6. Add the potatoes with the tomato paste and stir.
7. Add the cilantro, cover the pot, and cook for 10-15 minutes on medium low heat.
8. Allow to cook until the liquid has reduced and the oil has surfaced to the top. The sauce should've thickened at this point.
9. Serve with Chalau.

## ***Quarma Murgh (Chicken)***

1 lb. of skinless chicken breast and thigh pieces
1 large onion (sliced)
3-4 tablespoons of oil
¼ cup dal nakhud (soaked in advance)
2-3 tablespoons tomato paste
2-3 cloves of garlic (minced)
1-2 tablespoons coriander
1 teaspoon turmeric
1 teaspoon ginger (ground or fresh)
Salt (to taste)
Pepper (to taste)
4-5 Alou Bukhara (Bukhara plums)
1-2 whole jalapeno peppers (optional)
2-3 cups of water

1. In a sauce pan, heat the oil and caramelize the onions until light golden brown.
2. Add the chicken and stir with the onion for 3-5 minutes.
3. Add water along with the tomato paste, turmeric, coriander, garlic, ginger, salt, pepper, Alou Bukhara, and jalapeno peppers. Bring to a boil

4. Reduce the heat to medium high, cover the pan, and allow to simmer for 15-20 minutes.
5. In a separate pot, cook the dal nakhud with 2 cups of water on medium low heat for 7-10 minutes.
6. Drain the water once the dal nakhud softens and add to the quarma.
7. Cook for an additional 5-7 minutes on medium high heat. Cook until the liquid has reduced and the oil has surfaced to the top. The sauce should've thickened at this point.
8. Serve with Chalau.

## *Quarma Sabzi (Spinach)*

2-3 cups meat yakhnee
1 package of frozen spinach or 2 cups fresh chopped Spinach
1 tablespoon of holba
½ onion (sliced)
2-3 tablespoons of oil
1-2 tablespoon coriander
1 teaspoon turmeric
½ cup chopped gundana (or leeks)
½ cup chopped cilantro
2-3 cloves of garlic (minced)
½ teaspoon dill (dry)
1 whole jalapeno pepper (optional)
¼ cup black eyed beans (soaked in advance)
1 teaspoon ginger (fresh grated or ground)

1. Prepare the meat yakhnee and set aside.
2. In a separate pot, heat the oil and caramelize the onions until light golden brown.
3. Add the meat yakhnee along with the black eyed beans. Cover the pot and cook on medium heat for 5-10 minutes.
4. Add the spinach, cilantro, gundana, turmeric, coriander, dill, whole jalapeno peppers, holba, salt, pepper, and ginger. Stir.

5. Cover the pot and cook on medium low for 15-20 minutes. Once the water has reduced and the oil has surfaced, the quarma is ready.
6. Serve with Chalau.

*Quarma Sabzi with meat*

## Quarma Lubia Khushk (Dry Bean)

2-3 cups meat yakhnee
1 cup of dry kidney or black eyed beans (soaked in advance for at least 3 hours)
½ cup of oil
1 onion (sliced)
1-2 whole jalapeno peppers (optional)
1 teaspoon of turmeric
2-3 tablespoons of tomato paste
2-3 cloves of garlic (minced)
1 teaspoon ginger (fresh grated or ground)
1-2 tablespoon coriander
½ teaspoon of baking soda (optional)
Salt (to taste)
Pepper (to taste)
Water

1. Prepare the meat yakhnee and set aside.
2. In a separate pot, boil the beans until they are cooked (if using a pressure cooker, cook the beans for 10 minutes). Baking soda can be used to speed up the cooking process if a pressure cooker is not used.
3. In a separate pot, heat the oil and caramelize the onions until light golden brown.
4. Add the beans to the onion along with the meat yakhnee.
5. Add the whole jalapeno peppers, turmeric, ginger, coriander, and tomato puree. Cover the pot and cook on medium low heat for 15-20 minutes. Cook until the liquid has reduced and the oil has surfaced to the top. The sauce should've thickened at this point.
6. Serve with Chalau.

## *Quarma Samaruq (Mushroom)*

2-3 cups meat yakhnee
1 cup mushrooms
2-3 tablespoons of oil
1-2 jalapeno peppers (optional)
1 teaspoon of turmeric
2-3 tablespoons of tomato paste
1 teaspoon ginger (fresh grated or ground)
2 cloves of garlic (minced)
1-2 tablespoon coriander
Salt (to taste)
Pepper (to taste)
1-2 cups of water

1. Prepare the meat yakhnee and set aside.
2. In a separate pot, heat the oil and caramelize the onions until light golden brown.

3. Add the meat yakhnee along with the turmeric, garlic, coriander, ginger, salt, pepper, and tomato paste. Bring to a boil.
4. Wash the mushrooms and add to the quarma along with water.
5. Cover the pot and cook on medium low heat for 20 minutes. Cook until the liquid has reduced and the oil has surfaced to the top. The sauce should've thickened at this point.
6. Serve with Chalau.

## *Quarma Dal Nakhud and Alou Bukhara (split peas and plums)*

2-3 cups meat yakhnee
¼ cup dal nakhud (soaked in advance)
6-7 Alou Bukhara (Bukhara plums)
1 onion (sliced)
2-3 tablespoons of oil
1-2 jalapeno peppers (optional)
1 teaspoon turmeric
2-3 cloves of garlic (minced)
2-3 tablespoons tomato paste
1 teaspoon ginger (fresh grated or ground)
2-3 tablespoon coriander
Salt (to taste)
Pepper (to taste)

1. Prepare the meat yakhnee and set aside.
2. In a separate pot, heat the oil and caramelize the onions until light golden brown.
3. Add the meat yakhnee along with the turmeric, garlic, coriander, ginger, salt, pepper, and tomato paste. Bring to a boil.

4. Reduce the heat to medium low and add the plums and whole jalapeno peppers.
5. Cover the pot and cook on medium low heat for 10-15 more minutes.
6. In a separate pot, cook the dal nakhud with 2 cups of water on medium low heat for 7-10 minutes.
7. Drain the water once the dal nakhud softens and add to the quarma.
8. Cook for an additional 5-7 minutes on medium low heat. Cook until the liquid has reduced and the oil has surfaced to the top. The sauce should've thickened at this point.
9. Serve with Chalau.

## *Quarma Bamia (Okra)*

2-3 cups meat yakhnee
½ pound of Okra
3-4 large potatoes (optional)
½ onion (sliced)
2-3 tablespoons of tomato paste
1-2 jalapeno peppers
½ cup oil
1 teaspoon turmeric
1-2 cloves of garlic (minced)
1 teaspoon ginger (fresh grated or ground)
1-2 tablespoon coriander
½ cup of fresh chopped cilantro (optional)
Salt (to taste)
Pepper (to taste)

1. Prepare the meat yakhnee and set aside.
2. Wash the okra and cut the ends.
3. Lay cut okra out on a paper towel for 10-15 minutes until dry.

4. In a skillet, heat 2-3 tablespoons of oil and lightly sauté the okra.
5. In a saucepan, heat 2-3 tablespoons of oil and caramelize the onions until light golden brown.
6. Add the meat yakhnee to the onions along with the turmeric, coriander, garlic, salt, pepper, and ginger. Bring to a boil.
7. Peel and cut the potatoes in quarters and add to the quarma (optional).
8. Add the sautéed okra along with the tomato paste and stir.
9. Add the cilantro and stir (optional).
10. Add whole jalapeno peppers (optional).
11. Cover the pot and cook on medium heat for 10-15 minutes. Cook until the liquid has reduced and the oil has surfaced to the top. The sauce should've thickened at this point.
12. Serve with Chalau.

## Quarma Gul-e-Karam (Cauliflower)

2-3 cups meat yakhnee
½ pound of cauliflower
½ onion (sliced)
2-3 tablespoons of oil
2-3 tablespoons of tomato paste
1-2 jalapeno peppers (optional)
1 teaspoon turmeric
1-2 cloves of garlic (minced)
1 teaspoon ginger (fresh grated)
1-2 tablespoon coriander
Salt (to taste)
Pepper (to taste)
1-2 cups of water

1. Prepare the meat yakhnee and set aside.
2. In a separate pot, heat the oil and caramelize the onions until light golden brown.
3. Add the meat yakhnee along with the turmeric, garlic, coriander, ginger, salt, pepper, and tomato paste. Bring to a boil.
4. Separate cauliflower crowns and wash thoroughly.
5. Add the cauliflower crowns to the quarma and stir.
6. Cover the pot and cook on medium heat for 10-15 minutes.
7. In a separate pot, cook the dal nakhud with 2 cups of water on medium low heat for 7-10 minutes.
8. Drain the water once the dal nakhud softens and add to the quarma. Cook for an additional 5-7 minutes. Cook until the liquid has reduced and the oil has surfaced to the top. The sauce should've thickened at this point.
9. Serve with Chalau.

## *Quarma Shalghum (Turnips)*

2-3 cups meat yakhnee
1 pound of turnips
2-3 tablespoons of oil
½ onion (sliced)
1 teaspoon of ginger (fresh grated)
1 tablespoon tomato paste
2-3 cloves of garlic (minced)
1-2 jalapeno peppers
1 teaspoon turmeric
1-2 tablespoon coriander
Salt (to taste)
3 tablespoons of table sugar
1-2 cups of water

1. Prepare the meat yakhnee and set aside.
2. In a separate pot, heat the oil and caramelize the onions until light golden brown.
3. Add the meat yakhnee along with the turmeric, garlic, coriander, ginger, salt, whole jalapeno peppers, and tomato paste. Bring to a boil.
4. Wash and peel the turnips.
5. Cut the turnips in quarters and add to the quarma along with 1-2 cups of water and sugar.
6. Cover the pot and cook for 15-20 minutes or until turnip is cooked. Cook until the liquid has reduced and the oil has surfaced to the top. The sauce should've thickened at this point.
7. Serve with Chalau.

## *Quarma Zardak (Carrots)*

2-3 cups meat yakhnee
5-6 carrots
½ onion (sliced)
2-3 tablespoons of oil
1-2 cloves of garlic (minced)
1 teaspoon of ginger (fresh grated or ground)
1 tablespoon tomato paste
1-2 jalapeno peppers
1 teaspoon turmeric
1-2 tablespoon coriander
Salt (to taste)
Pepper (to taste)
2 tablespoons of table sugar
1-2 cups of water

1. Prepare the meat yakhnee and set aside.

2. In a separate pot, heat the oil and caramelize the onions until light golden brown.
3. Add the meat yakhnee along with the turmeric, garlic, coriander, ginger, salt, whole jalapeno peppers, salt, pepper, and tomato paste. Bring to a boil.
4. Peel, cut, and slice the carrots.
5. Add the carrots to the quarma along with the sugar and water. Stir.
6. Cover the pot and cook for 20 minutes on medium heat. Cook until the liquid has reduced and the oil has surfaced to the top. The sauce should've thickened at this point.
7. Serve with Chalau.

## ***Quarma Banjan Rumi (Tomatoes)***

2-3 cups meat yakhnee
5-6 large tomatoes
½ onion (sliced)
2-3 tablespoons of oil
2-3 cloves of garlic (minced)
1-2 fresh jalapeno peppers
1 teaspoon of ginger (fresh grated or ground)
1-2 tablespoon coriander
1 teaspoon of turmeric
Salt (to taste)
Pepper (to taste)
1-2 cups of water

1. Prepare the meat yakhnee and set aside.
2. In a separate pot, heat the oil and caramelize the onions until light golden brown.
3. Add the meat yakhnee along with the turmeric, garlic, coriander, ginger, salt, pepper, and whole jalapeno peppers. Bring to a boil. Reduce heat to medium low and allow to simmer.

4. Place the tomatoes in a large deep bowl and add boiling water to the tomatoes.
5. Drain the boiling water and allow the tomatoes to cool prior to peeling the skin off.
6. Cut the peeled tomatoes in quarters and add to the quarma.
7. Cover the pot and cook on medium heat for 15-20 minutes. Cook until the liquid has reduced and the oil has surfaced to the top. The sauce should've thickened at this point.
8. Serve with Chalau.

## Quarma Fasilya (Green Bean)

2-3 cups meat yakhnee
1 pound of Green beans
½ onion (sliced)
2-3 tablespoons of oil
1-2 cloves of garlic (minced)
1-2 fresh jalapeno peppers
1-2 tablespoons of tomato paste
1 teaspoon of ginger (fresh grated or ground)
1-2 tablespoon coriander
1 teaspoon of turmeric
Salt (to taste)
Pepper (to taste)
1-2 cups of water

1. Prepare the meat yakhnee and set aside.
2. In a separate pot, heat the oil and caramelize the onions until light golden brown.
3. Add the meat yakhnee along with the turmeric, garlic, coriander, ginger, salt, pepper, whole jalapeno peppers, and tomato paste. Bring to a boil.
4. Wash the green beans and cut the ends.

5. Add the green beans to the beef quarma along with water. Cook in a covered pot for 15-20 minutes on medium low heat. Cook until the liquid has reduced and the oil has surfaced to the top. The sauce should've thickened at this point.
6. Serve with Chalau.

## *Quarma Banjan (Eggplant)*

2-3 cups meat yakhnee
1-2 Eggplant (peeled and cut in large chunks)
½ onion (sliced)
2-3 tablespoons of oil
1-2 cloves of garlic (minced)
1-2 tablespoons tomato paste
1-2 fresh jalapeno peppers
1 teaspoon of ginger (fresh grated or ground)
1-2 tablespoon coriander
1 teaspoon of turmeric
Salt (to taste)
Pepper (to taste)
1-2 cups of water

1. Prepare the meat yakhnee and set aside.
2. In a separate pot, heat the oil and caramelize the onions until light golden brown.
3. Add the meat yakhnee along with the turmeric, garlic, coriander, ginger, salt, pepper, whole jalapeno peppers, and tomato paste. Bring to a boil.
4. Add the eggplant chunks to the quarma along with water.
5. Cover the pot and cook on medium low heat for 15-20 minutes. Cook until the liquid has reduced and the oil has surfaced to the top. The sauce should've thickened at this point.

6. Serve with Chalau.

# *Curry Quarma*

2-3 cups meat yakhnee
½ onion (sliced)
2-3 tablespoons of oil
1-2 jalapeno peppers
1-2 cloves of garlic (minced)
1 teaspoon of turmeric
1-2 tablespoons of tomato paste
1 tablespoon of curry powder
2 tablespoon of white flour
1 teaspoon ginger (fresh grated or ground)
1-2 tablespoon coriander
2 jalapeno peppers
Salt (to taste)
Pepper (to taste)
1-2 cups of water

1. Prepare the meat yakhnee and set aside.
2. In a separate pot, heat the oil and caramelize the onions until light golden brown.
3. Add the meat yakhnee along with the turmeric, garlic, coriander, ginger, salt, whole jalapeno peppers, and tomato paste. Bring to a boil.
4. In a separate bowl, mix the curry powder and the flour with ½ cup of water.
5. Add the curry mixture along with an additional ½ cup of water to the quarma and stir.
6. Cover the pot and cook on medium low heat for 10-15 minutes. Cook until the liquid has reduced and the oil has surfaced to the top. The sauce should've thickened at this point.
7. Serve with Chalau.

# ***Cherry Quarma***

2-3 cups meat yakhnee
1 pound fresh pitted cherries
½ onion (sliced)
2-3 tablespoons of oil
1-2 cloves of garlic (minced)
1 tablespoon tomato paste
2 tablespoons of sugar
1-2 jalapeno peppers
¼ teaspoon of chili powder
1-2 cardamom seeds (whole)
1 teaspoon ginger (fresh grated or ground)
Salt (to taste)
Pepper (to taste)
1-2 cups of water

1. Prepare the meat yakhnee and set aside.
2. In a separate pot, heat the oil and caramelize the onions until light golden brown.
3. Add the meat yakhnee along with the water, turmeric, garlic, coriander, cherries, sugar, cardamom seeds, chili powder, ginger, salt, pepper, whole jalapeno peppers, and tomato paste. Bring to a boil.
4. Cover the pot and cook on medium heat for 10-15 minutes. Cook until the liquid has reduced and the oil has surfaced to the top. The sauce should've thickened at this point.
5. Serve with Chalau.

# Quarma Seb Taza (Fresh Apples)

2-3 cups meat yakhnee
2-3 large Granny Smith Apples
½ onion (sliced)
2-3 tablespoons of oil
1-2 cloves of garlic (minced)
1-2 jalapeno peppers
1 teaspoon of turmeric
1 tablespoon of tomato paste
1 teaspoon ginger (fresh grated or ground)
1-2 tablespoon coriander
Salt (to taste)
Pepper (to taste)
1-2 cups of water

1. Prepare the meat yakhnee and set aside.
2. In a separate pot, heat the oil and caramelize the onions until light golden brown.
3. Add the meat yakhnee along with the turmeric, garlic, coriander, ginger, salt, pepper, whole jalapeno peppers, and tomato paste. Bring to a boil.
4. Peel and cut the apples into quarters prior to adding to the quarma along with 1-2 cups of water.
5. Cover the pot and cook for 20 minutes on medium heat. Cook until the liquid has reduced and the oil has surfaced to the top. The sauce should've thickened at this point.
6. Serve with Chalau.

# ***Basic Ground Meat Sauce***

*This is the base for many dishes such as spaghetti, Kitchiree Quroot, Aushak, Mantu, and Aush. Vegetables such as peas can be added to this base to make a regular quarma. The base can be prepared ahead of time and put in the freezer for future use.*

1 large onion (finely chopped)
1 lb. of ground beef or turkey
2-3 tablespoons of oil
2-3 tablespoons of tomato paste
1-2 tablespoon coriander
1 teaspoon turmeric
Salt (to taste)
Pepper (to taste)
½ teaspoon ginger (fresh grated or ground)
¼ cup dal nakhud (pre-washed and soaked)
2-3 cloves of garlic (minced)
1-2 cups of water

1. In a sauce pan, heat the oil and sauté the onions until they are transparent.
2. Add the ground meat and stir until browned.
3. Add the water along with the tomato paste, garlic, coriander, turmeric, salt, pepper, and ginger. Mix well.
4. In a separate pot, cook the dal nakhud with 2 cups of water on medium low heat for 10 minutes.
5. Cover the pot and cook on low to medium heat for 15-20 minutes.
6. Drain the water once the dal nakhud softens and add to the sauce base.
7. Cook for an additional 3-5 minutes.

# Kohfta (Meatballs)

*When I used to eat beef, this was one of my favorite dishes. I have since discovered how to make this using ground turkey. The turkey version tastes very similar to the delicious meatballs I remember. This dish is much easier to cook with a pressure cooker when using beef.*

1 pound ground beef or turkey
3-4 tablespoons of oil
2 large onions
2-3 tablespoons of tomato paste
¼ cup of dal nakhud (washed and soaked in advance)
6-7 cloves of garlic (minced)
10-15 Alou Bukhara (optional)
1 teaspoon black pepper
1-2 teaspoons salt
1-2 fresh jalapeno peppers (optional)
2 teaspoons of turmeric
2 teaspoons of ginger (fresh grated or ground)
3-4 tablespoons of coriander
Water

1. Finely chop 1 onion and set aside.
2. In a large bowl mix the ground meat, chopped onions, 3-4 cloves of minced garlic, ½ teaspoon of black pepper, 2 tablespoons coriander, 1 teaspoon ginger, 1 teaspoon turmeric, and salt.
3. Mix the meat, onions, and spices really well; use hands if necessary.
4. Make tight ping-pong size balls with your hands and set on a plate.
5. Add 6-8 cups of water in a pot and bring to a boil. Gently place the meatballs in the boiling water and boil for 5 minutes.

6. Remove the meatballs from the water and set aside. Do not jam all the meatballs in at once. Cook several at a time for 5 minutes each.
7. Slice the remaining onion.
8. Heat the oil in a pressure cooker on high heat. Reduce the heat to medium high and caramelize the sliced onions until light golden brown.
9. Once the onions are caramelized, add the meatballs with 2-3 cups of water.
10. Add 1 additional teaspoon of turmeric and ginger, 1-2 additional tablespoons of coriander, the remaining 2-3 cloves of minced garlic as well as salt and pepper.
11. Add the tomato paste, jalapeno peppers, and Alou Bukhara (optional); mix well.
12. For beef meatballs, fasten the pressure cooker lid and pressure cook for 10 minutes. For turkey meatballs, place a cover on the pressure cooker or regular pot and cook on medium low for 15-20 minutes.
13. In a separate pot, cook the dal nakhud with 2 cups of water on medium low heat for 7-10 minutes.
14. Drain the water once the dal nakhud softens and add to the quarma.
15. Cook for an additional 5-7 minutes on medium high heat. Cook until the water has reduced and the oil has surfaced to the top.
16. Serve with Chalau.

*Kohfta Quarma (Turkey)*

Vegetarian
Quarma

# Kachaloo Quarma (Potatoes)

2-3 tablespoons of oil
2 large potatoes
1 onion (sliced)
2 cloves of garlic (minced)
2-3 tablespoons of tomato paste
1 fresh jalapeno pepper
Salt (to taste)
Black pepper (to taste)
1 teaspoon ginger (fresh grated or ground)
2-3 tablespoon coriander
1 teaspoon turmeric
½ cup chopped cilantro
1-2 cups of water

1. Heat the oil on medium high heat and caramelize the sliced onions until light golden brown.
2. Peel and cut the potatoes into medium size chunks and sauté with the onion for 2-3 minutes.
3. Add the water along with the tomato paste, minced garlic, salt, pepper, ginger, turmeric, coriander, and fresh jalapeno pepper. Stir. Cover the pot and allow to cook on medium low heat for 10-15 minutes.
4. Add the cilantro and allow to cook for an additional 5 minutes. Cook until the water has reduced and the oil has surfaced to the top.
5. Serve with Chalau.

# Quarma Lubia (Kidney Beans)

*This is my aunt Khurshaid's favorite dish and her creation.*

1 can of red kidney beans
½ onion (finely chopped)
2-3 tablespoons of oil
2-3 tablespoon coriander
Salt (to taste)
Ground red chili pepper to taste
1 teaspoon turmeric
3-4 cloves of garlic (minced)
1 teaspoon ground cumin
1-2 tablespoons tomato sauce
Crushed dried mint (optional)
1-2 cups of water

1. Drain and rinse the kidney beans and set aside.
2. Heat the oil on medium high heat and caramelize the onions until light golden brown.
3. Add the beans, water, coriander, salt, pepper, turmeric, garlic, cumin, and tomato sauce. Stir.
4. Cover the pot and cook on medium heat for about 15-20 minutes. Cook until the water has reduced and the oil has surfaced to the top.
5. Once ready, mix in crushed dried mint (optional but tastes good with it).
6. Serve with Chalau.

# *Quarma Sabzi (Spinach)*

1 package of frozen spinach or 2 cups fresh chopped Spinach
2-3 tablespoons of oil
½ onion (finely chopped)
1 tablespoon of holba
2-3 tablespoon coriander
1 teaspoon turmeric
½ cup chopped gundana (or leeks)
½ cup chopped cilantro
1 jalapeno pepper
¼ cup black eyed beans
½ teaspoon dill
2-3 cloves of garlic (minced)
1 teaspoon ginger (fresh grated or ground)
Salt and pepper to taste
1-1 ½ cup of water

1. Heat the oil on medium high heat and caramelize the onions until light golden brown.
2. Add the water, black eyed beans, salt, and pepper. Cover the pot and cook for 10 minutes.
3. Lower the heat and add the spinach, cilantro, and gundana, along with the coriander, turmeric, dill, garlic, whole jalapeno pepper, holba, and ginger. Stir.
4. Cover the pot and cook on medium low for 10-15 minutes. Cook until the water has reduced and the oil has surfaced to the top.
5. Serve with Chalau.

# *Quarma Bamia (Okra)*

1 medium onion (sliced)
½ pound of okra
¼ cup of oil
2 large potatoes (optional)
Salt (to taste)
Black pepper (to taste)
2 cloves of garlic (minced)
2-3 tablespoons of tomato paste
1-2 jalapeno peppers
1 teaspoon ginger (fresh grated or ground)
2-3 tablespoon coriander
½ cup of fresh chopped cilantro (optional)
2-3 cups of water

1. Wash the okra and cut the ends.
2. Lay cut okra out on a paper towel for 10-15 minutes until dry.
3. In a skillet, heat 1-2 tablespoons of oil and lightly sauté the okra.
4. In a medium pot, heat 2-3 tablespoons of oil and caramelize the onions until light golden brown.
5. Add the water and bring to a boil.
6. Add the garlic, salt, pepper, turmeric, coriander, and ginger.
7. Peel and cut the potatoes in quarters and add to the quarma (optional).
8. Add the okra along with the tomato paste and stir.
9. Add the cilantro and stir (optional).
10. Add the whole jalapeno peppers.
11. Cover the pot and cook on medium heat for 10-15 minutes. Cook until the water has reduced and the oil has surfaced to the top.
12. Serve with Chalau.

# *Quarma Gul-e-Karam (Cauliflower)*

½ pound of cauliflower
1 medium onion (sliced)
2-3 tablespoons of oil
Salt (to taste)
Black pepper (to taste)
2 cloves of garlic (minced)
¼ cup dal nakhud (soaked in advance)
2-3 tablespoons of tomato paste
1-2 jalapeno peppers
1 teaspoon turmeric
1 teaspoon ginger (fresh grated or ground)
2-3 tablespoon coriander
1-2 cups of water

1. In a medium pot, heat the oil and sauté the onion until golden brown.
2. Add the water and bring to a boil.
3. Separate the cauliflower crowns and wash thoroughly.
4. Add the cauliflower crowns to the quarma. Add an additional cup of water as needed.
5. Add fresh ginger, turmeric, tomato paste, whole jalapeno peppers, garlic, salt, pepper, and coriander.
6. Cover the pot and cook on medium heat for 10-15 minutes.
7. In a separate pot, cook the dal nakhud with 2 cups of water on medium low heat for 10 minutes.
8. Drain the water once the dal nakhud softens and add to the quarma.
9. Cook for an additional 5 minutes. Cook until the water has reduced and the oil has surfaced to the top.
10. Serve with Chalau.

## Quarma Shalghum (Turnips)

1 pound of turnips
1 teaspoon of fresh grated ginger
Salt (to taste)
Black pepper (to taste)
2 cloves of garlic (minced)
1 tablespoon tomato paste
1-2 jalapeno peppers
1 teaspoon turmeric
2-3 tablespoon coriander
3 tablespoons of table sugar
1-2 cups of water

1. Slice the onion.
2. In a medium pot, heat the oil and sauté the onion until golden brown.
3. Add the water and bring to a boil.
4. Wash and peel the turnips. Cut turnips in quarters and add to the onions along with fresh grated ginger, tomato paste, garlic, salt, pepper, turmeric, coriander, whole jalapeno peppers, and sugar.
5. Cover the pot and cook for 15-20 minutes on medium heat. Cook until the water has reduced and the oil has surfaced to the top.
6. Serve with Chalau.

## Quarma Zardak (Carrots)

5-6 carrots
2-3 tablespoons of oil
1 medium onion (sliced)
Salt (to taste)
Black pepper (to taste)
2 tablespoons of table sugar

2 cloves of garlic (minced)
1 tablespoon tomato paste
1 teaspoon ginger (fresh grated or ground)
1-2 jalapeno peppers
1 teaspoon turmeric
1-2 tablespoon coriander
2-3 cups of water

1. In a medium pot, heat the oil and sauté the onion until golden brown.
2. Add the water and bring to a boil.
3. Peel, cut, and slice the carrots and add to the quarma along with the garlic, sugar, salt, pepper, ginger, tomato paste, turmeric, and coriander.
4. Cover the pot and cook for 20 minutes on medium heat. Cook until the water has reduced and the oil has surfaced to the top.
5. Serve with Chalau.

## ***Quarma Banjan Rumi (Tomatoes)***

5-6 large tomatoes
2-3 tablespoons of oil
1 large onion (sliced)
¼ cup of dal nakhud (soaked in advance)
2 cloves of garlic (minced)
1-2 fresh jalapeno peppers
1 teaspoon of ginger (fresh grated or ground)
Salt (to taste)
Black pepper (to taste)
2-3 tablespoons of coriander
1 teaspoon turmeric
2-3 cups of water

1. In a medium pot, heat the oil and sauté the onion until golden brown.
2. Add the water and bring to a boil.
3. Place the tomatoes in a deep bowl and add boiling water to the tomatoes.
4. Drain the boiling water and allow the tomatoes to cool prior to peeling the skin off.
5. Cut the peeled tomatoes in quarters and add to the onions.
6. Add the whole jalapeno peppers, garlic, salt, pepper, turmeric, coriander, and ginger.
7. Cover the pot and cook on medium heat for 15-20 minutes.
8. In a separate pot, cook the dal nakhud with 2 cups of water on medium low heat for 10 minutes.
9. Drain the water once the dal nakhud softens and add to the quarma. Cook for an additional 5 minutes. Cook until the water has reduced and the oil has surfaced to the top.
10. Serve with Chalau.

## *Quarma Fasilya (Green Bean)*

1 pound of green beans
2-3 tablespoons of oil
1 medium onion (sliced)
2 cloves of garlic (minced)
1-2 fresh jalapeno peppers
1 teaspoon of ginger (fresh grated or ground)
Salt (to taste)
Black pepper (to taste)
1-2 tablespoons tomato paste
2-3 tablespoons coriander
1 teaspoon turmeric
2-3 cups of water

1. Wash the green beans and cut the ends.

2. In a medium pot, heat the oil and sauté the onion until golden brown.
3. Add the water and bring to a boil.
4. Add the green beans to the onions along with the garlic, ginger, salt, pepper, coriander, tomato paste, turmeric, and whole jalapeno peppers.
5. Cover the pot and cook on medium heat for 10-15 minutes. Cook until the water has reduced and the oil has surfaced to the top.
6. Serve with Chalau.

## ***Quarma Banjan (Eggplant)***

1-2 eggplant
2-3 tablespoons of oil
1 medium onion (sliced)
2 cloves of garlic (minced)
2 fresh jalapeno peppers
1 teaspoon ginger (fresh grated or ground)
1-2 tablespoons tomato paste
Salt (to taste)
Pepper (to taste)
2-3 tablespoons coriander
1 teaspoon of turmeric
1-2 cups of water

1. In a medium pot, heat the oil and sauté the onion until golden brown.
2. Add the water and bring to a boil.
3. Peel the eggplant and cut in chunks.
4. Add the eggplant to the onions along with the garlic, tomato paste, ginger, salt, pepper, coriander, turmeric, and whole jalapeno peppers.
5. Cover the pot and cook on medium heat for 15-20 minutes. Cook until the water has reduced and the oil has surfaced to the top.

6. Serve with Chalau.

## Quarma Samaruq (Mushroom)

1 cup of mushrooms
2-3 tablespoons of oil
1 medium onion (sliced)
Salt (to taste)
Black pepper (to taste)
1-2 jalapeno peppers
1 teaspoon of turmeric
2-3 tablespoons of tomato paste
1 teaspoon ginger (fresh grated or ground)
2 cloves of garlic (minced)
2-3 tablespoons of coriander
1-2 cups of water

1. In a medium pot, heat the oil and sauté the onion until golden brown.
2. Thoroughly wash the mushrooms and add to the onions. Stir with the onions for 5 minutes.
3. Add the water along with the garlic, turmeric, coriander, ginger, salt, tomato paste, whole jalapeno peppers, and black pepper.
4. Cover the pot and cook for 20 minutes on medium low heat. Cook until the water has reduced and the oil has surfaced to the top.
5. Serve with Chalau.

## Quarma Samaruq with Mahst (Mushroom with yogurt)

*I first ate this quarma at my cousin Hasina's house and loved it. I love the combination of the mushroom with the yogurt in a quarma sauce.*

1 lb. whole button or crimini mushrooms
¼ cup of oil
1 small onion (finely chopped)
2-3 cloves of garlic (minced)
1 teaspoon turmeric
1-2 tablespoons coriander
½ cup of fresh cilantro (chopped)
Salt (to taste)
Pepper (to taste)
1-2 whole jalapeno peppers
1 cup plain mahst (yogurt)
1 cup water

1. In a medium pot, heat the oil and sauté the onion until golden brown.
2. Thoroughly wash the mushrooms, remove the stem, and cut in quarters.
3. Add the mushrooms to the onions.
4. Add the garlic, turmeric, coriander, cilantro, salt, and black pepper. Sauté until the mushrooms are lightly browned.
5. Add the water along with the whole jalapeno peppers and allow to cook on medium low heat for 10-15 minutes.
6. Mix in the yogurt and cook on medium heat for an additional 5 minutes
7. Serve with Chalau.

## ***Quarma Dal Nakhud and Alou Bukhara (Split Peas and Plums)***

¼ cup of dal nakhud (soaked in advance)
6-7 Alou Bukhara (Bukhara plums)
2-3 tablespoons of oil
1 medium onion (sliced)
Salt (to taste)
Black pepper (to taste)
1-2 jalapeno peppers
1 teaspoon of turmeric
2-3 tablespoons of tomato paste
1 teaspoon ginger (fresh grated or ground)
2 cloves of garlic (minced)
2-3 tablespoons coriander
2-3 cups of water

1. In a medium pot, heat the oil and sauté the onion until golden brown.
2. Add the water and bring to a boil.
3. Add the garlic, turmeric, coriander, ginger, salt, and pepper.
4. Add the tomato paste along with the alou bukhara and whole jalapeno peppers.
5. Cover the pot and cook for 5-7 minutes on medium low heat.
6. In a separate pot, cook the dal nakhud with 2 cups of water on medium low heat for 10 minutes.
7. Drain the water once the dal nakhud softens and add to the quarma. Cook together for an additional 5 minutes.
8. Serve with Chalau.

# Curry Quarma

2-3 tablespoons of oil
1 medium onion (sliced)
Salt (to taste)
Black pepper (to taste)
1-2 jalapeno peppers
1 teaspoon of turmeric
2-3 tablespoons of tomato paste
1 tablespoon of curry powder
2 tablespoon of white flour
1 teaspoon ginger (fresh grated or ground)
2 cloves of garlic (minced)
1-2 tablespoon coriander
2-3 cups of water

1. In a medium pot, heat the oil and sauté the onion until golden brown.
2. Add the water and bring to a boil.
3. Add tomato paste with a cup of water and boil for 5 minutes and stir occasionally.
4. Add garlic, turmeric, coriander, ginger, salt, and pepper.
5. In a separate bowl, mix the curry powder and the flour with ½ cup of water.
6. Add the curry mixture to the quarma and stir.
7. Add the whole jalapeno peppers with an additional ½ cup of water.
8. Cover the pot and cook for 10-15 minutes on medium low heat. Cook until the water has reduced and the oil has surfaced to the top.
9. Serve with Chalau.

## Cherry Quarma

2-3 tablespoons of oil
1 pound fresh pitted cherries
2 tablespoons of sugar
1 medium onion (sliced)
Salt (to taste)
1-2 jalapeno peppers
½ teaspoon of chili powder
1-2 cardamom seeds (whole)
1 teaspoon ginger (fresh grated or ground)
2-3 cups of water

1. In a medium pot, heat the oil and sauté the onion until golden brown.
2. Add the water and bring to a boil.
3. Add the cherries, ginger, sugar, cardamom seeds, whole jalapeno peppers, and chili powder to the quarma.
4. Cover the pot and cook for 15-20 minutes on medium low heat. Cook until the water has reduced and the oil has surfaced to the top.
5. Serve with Chalau.

## Quarma Seb Taza (Fresh Apples)

2-3 large Granny Smith apples
2-3 tablespoons of oil
1 medium onion (sliced)
Salt (to taste)
Black pepper (to taste)
1-2 jalapeno peppers
1 teaspoon of turmeric
1 tablespoon tomato paste
1 teaspoon ginger (fresh grated or ground)

1-2 tablespoon coriander
2-3 cups of water

1. In a medium pot, heat the oil and sauté the onion until golden brown.
2. Add the water and bring to a boil.
3. Add the minced garlic, turmeric, coriander, ginger, salt, and pepper.
4. Peel and cut the apples into quarters prior to adding to the quarma.
5. Add the tomato paste and whole jalapeno peppers. Stir.
6. Cover the pot and cook for 20 minutes on medium low heat. Cook until the water has reduced and the oil has surfaced to the top.
7. Serve with Chalau.

# Fish

Afghans usually prepare fish as either kabobs, fried, or as a quarma. With the exception of the quarma recipe, the recipes below are not traditional Afghan recipes. The fish recipe's I've included are a variation of recipes that have evolved in our household over the years.

## Salmon

*This recipe came about in my moment of experimentation in the kitchen and it has since become a family favorite. My favorite way to eat this dish is with brown rice and steamed vegetables. It's also good with chalau.*

*With Salmon, it's important to understand the difference between wild salmon and farmed salmon (Atlantic Salmon). I prefer the wild Alaskan Salmon or Sockeye Salmon and avoid anything that has been farmed.*

3-4 fillets of skinless salmon
1 large onion (sliced)
2-3 tablespoons of oil
2 large tomatoes

Marinade:
4-5 cloves of garlic (minced)
1 lemon (juiced)
1-2 tablespoons coriander
1 teaspoon ginger (fresh grated or ground)
Salt (to taste)
Black pepper (to taste)
2-3 big tablespoons of plain yogurt

1. Rinse the salmon under cold water.
2. In a deep dish mix the yogurt, lemon juice, garlic, salt, pepper, and coriander.

3. Place the salmon, one fillet at a time, and thoroughly turn in the marinade until all the fish is covered.
4. Marinate for at least ½ hour in the fridge. The longer the better.
5. In a skillet, heat the oil and sauté the onion until golden brown.
6. Add the fish along with the marinade.
7. Chop the tomatoes and add to the fish.
8. Cover and cook on low heat for 10-15 minutes.
9. Serve with Chalau (or brown rice) and steamed vegetables.

## ***Bowtie Pasta, Black Beans, and Salmon***

3-4 fillets of skinless salmon
1 large onion (sliced)
2-3 tablespoons of oil
2 large tomatoes
1 can of black beans
1 bag of bowtie pasta

Marinade:
4-5 cloves of garlic (minced)
1 lemon (juiced)
1-2 tablespoons coriander
1 teaspoon ginger (fresh grated or ground)
Salt (to taste)
Black pepper (to taste)
2-3 big tablespoons of plain yogurt

1. Rinse the salmon under cold water.
2. In a deep dish mix the yogurt, lemon juice, garlic, salt, pepper, and coriander.
3. Place the salmon, one fillet at a time, and thoroughly turn in the marinade until all the fish is covered.

4. Marinate for at least ½ hour in the fridge. The longer the better.
5. In a skillet, heat the oil and sauté the onion until golden brown.
6. Add the fish along with the marinade.
7. Chop the tomatoes and add to the fish.
8. Rinse the black beans and add to the fish.
9. Cover the skillet and cook the fish on medium low heat for 10-15 minutes.
10. In the meantime, boil some water for the pasta.
11. Add a pinch of salt to the boiling water and add the bowtie pasta.
12. Cook the pasta until it is al dente.
13. Drain the pasta and put back in the pot.
14. In a big pasta serving dish, mix the cooked pasta and fish to thoroughly coat the pasta.
15. Serve.

## *Salmon with Mushrooms & Asparagus*

3-4 fillets of skinless salmon
¼ cup of oil
2 cups sliced mushrooms
1 onion (chopped)
1 teaspoon marjoram
2-3 cloves of garlic (minced)
1 cup vegetable stock
2 cups asparagus (cut into 1 ½ inch pieces)
1 cup cherry tomatoes (cut in half)
1 lemon (juiced)
Salt (to taste)
Pepper (to taste)
¼ cup fresh flat leaved parsley (chopped)

1. Rinse the salmon under cold water, dry with paper towels, and season with salt and pepper.
2. In a large skillet, heat 2-3 tablespoons of oil and add the mushrooms. Sauté mushrooms for about 5 minutes.
3. Add the onion and garlic and cook for an additional 7-10 minutes.
4. Add the vegetable broth and bring to a boil.
5. Reduce the heat and allow the mushrooms to simmer on medium low heat for 10-15 minutes.
6. Add the asparagus. Cover the skillet and cook for 3-4 minutes.
7. Add the tomatoes, parsley, lemon juice, salt, and pepper and cook an additional 5 minutes on medium heat.
8. In another skillet, heat 2-3 tablespoons of oil and add the salmon. Cover the pot and cook until Salmon is flakey and pink on the inside.
9. Transfer the mushroom mix onto a platter.
10. Place the salmon next to the vegetables and serve.

## *Quarma Mahi (Fish)*

1 pound fish fillets (e.g. Mahi Mahi type of fish)
½ cup of oil
1 medium onion (sliced)
½ teaspoon of red chili powder
Salt
Pepper
1-2 tablespoon coriander
2-3 tablespoons of tomato paste
3 cloves of garlic (minced)
1 teaspoon ginger (fresh grated or ground)
1 teaspoon of turmeric
1-2 cups of water

1. Wash and cut fish in 3" chunks.

2. In a skillet, heat 3-4 tablespoons of oil and sauté the fish until lightly browned. Take the fish out of the oil and drain oil from the fish.
3. In a medium pot, heat 2-3 tablespoons of oil and sauté the onions until golden brown.
4. Add water along with the fish, tomato paste, coriander, ginger, chili powder, salt, pepper, garlic, and turmeric.
5. Cover the pot and cook for 10-15 minutes on medium low heat. Cook until the liquid has reduced and the oil has surfaced to the top. The sauce should've thickened at this point.
6. Serve with Chalau.

## Fish Skewers

*This recipe is a great alternative to hamburgers at a BBQ.*

2 lbs. firm textured fish steaks (swordfish, halibut, or cod)
2 bell peppers
1 lemon (juiced)
3 tablespoons oil
3-4 cloves of garlic (minced)
¼ teaspoon pepper

Salsa:
2 large tomatoes
1 medium onion (finely chopped)
¼ teaspoon of salt
1 teaspoon of sugar
1 tablespoon red wine vinegar

1. Cut the fish into 1-1 ½ inch chunks
2. Cut bell peppers in large chunks
3. Dice the tomatoes.

4. In a separate bowl mix the diced tomatoes, onions, salt, sugar, and vinegar. Cover and refrigerate the salsa for at least 30 minutes or until the next day.
5. In a deep bowl, combine the oil, garlic, lemon juice, and pepper. Add the fish chunks and turn to coat.
6. Thread the fish chunks and bell peppers equally spaced on metal skewers.
7. Place foil on the grill and then place the skewers. Poke holes in the foil and cook turning several times, until the fish begins to flake.
8. Top with salsa and serve.

## *Fish Baked with Tomatoes and Garlic*

2 lbs. firm textured fish (Cod, Halibut, or Mahi-Mahi fillets)
Salt
2 lemons (juiced)
2 onions (sliced)
2-3 cloves garlic (minced)
½ cup olive oil
4 tomatoes (chopped)
½ cup parsley (chopped)
1 teaspoon paprika
½ teaspoon sugar

1. Rinse the fish under cold water.
2. Place the fish in a deep dish and sprinkle it with a little salt and the juice of 1 lemon. Cover and set it aside for 30 minutes.
3. Sauté the onions and garlic lightly in a 2-3 tablespoons of oil.
4. Add the tomatoes and parsley to the onions and continue cooking for 2-3 minutes.

5. Add the paprika, salt, and sugar, and stir. Turn off the heat and set aside.
6. Transfer half the sautéed vegetables from the skillet to a glass baking dish.
7. Place the fish on top of the vegetables in the baking dish.
8. Spread the remaining vegetables over the fish.
9. Combine the ¼ cup of olive oil with the juice of the remaining lemon and pour all over the fish and vegetables.
10. Cover the glass dish and bake at 350° F for 30 minutes.
11. Uncover the dish and continue baking for 10 more minutes or until the fish is cooked all the way through.

# Kabobs

# *Chapli Kabob*

¼ -½ cup all purpose flour
1 lb. ground beef
1 onion
3-4 cloves of garlic (minced)
2-3 tablespoons of coriander
1-2 teaspoon ginger (fresh grated or ground)
1 teaspoon turmeric
½ teaspoon black pepper
¼ teaspoon red crushed pepper
1 teaspoon salt
¼ cup fresh cilantro (chopped)
3-4 tablespoons of oil

1. In a food processor, chop the onion.
2. In a bowl, mix the beef, flour, onion, garlic, coriander, turmeric, ginger, black pepper, red crushed pepper, salt, and cilantro. Knead the mix well.
3. Make the mixture into flat patties (like hamburgers).
4. In a skillet, add the oil and heat on high.
5. Reduce the heat to low, place the patties in the skillet, cover the skillet, and slowly cook until the patties are done (about 15-20 minutes). Watch the patties so they don't dry out.
6. Serve with other kabobs or make a hamburger sandwich out of it.

# ***Shami Kabob (A.K.A Lola Kabob)***

*This recipe belongs to my aunt Aquila. I don't eat beef but on several occasions, I have eaten 1-2 of these at dinner parties because they are so delicious. As a child I used to eat the ground beef mixture before the kabobs were fried because I loved the taste so much. I used to say that if I ever ate beef again, it would be for the shami kabobs.*

2 lbs. beef
3 potatoes
1 big onion (sliced)
4-5 cloves of garlic (minced)
1-2 tablespoons of coriander
1-2 teaspoon ginger (fresh grated or ground)
½ cup of fresh cilantro
3 eggs whites
1-2 cups of oil
Salt (to taste)
Black pepper
Water

1. Wash and cut beef into chunks.
2. In a saucepan, add the beef with the onion along with 3-4 cups of water. Cook on medium heat for 30-40 minutes or until well done.
3. Boil the potatoes separately until soft. Set aside and let cool.
4. Peel the potatoes and cut in quarters.
5. Once the meat is cooked, drain the water from the meat.
6. In a meat grinder, grind the meat, cilantro, and the potatoes.
7. Add the pepper, garlic, ginger, coriander, salt, turmeric, and egg whites to the meat and potato mixture. Mix the ingredients really well.

8. Take a small amount of the mixture and roll with your hands into small rolls.
9. Heat the oil in a deep skillet and fry the rolled meat until browned.
10. Serve.

# Chicken Kabob with Bell Peppers

*This is my aunt Khurshaid's specialty. She usually makes it for special dinner parties at her house and it's always a hit with everyone.*

2-3 chicken breasts cut into 1-inch cubes
2 lemons (juiced)
1-2 tablespoon coriander
1 teaspoon turmeric
Salt
1 teaspoon of ground red chili pepper
1 teaspoon of ginger (fresh grated or ground)
4-5 cloves of garlic (minced)
1-2 Green Bell Peppers (cut into small pieces)
2-3 Potatoes (peeled and chopped in small chunks)
2-3 tablespoons of oil
2 teaspoons of curry powder
½ cup cilantro (chopped)
2-3 cups of water

1. In a deep pot, add the chicken and oil, along with lemon juice, coriander, turmeric, salt, pepper, ginger, garlic, and water. Cover pot and cook for 5-10 minutes on medium heat.
2. Add the potatoes, mix well and cook for an additional 10-15 minutes. Add more water as needed.

3. Once the chicken and potatoes are done, add the curry powder, bell peppers, and cilantro and cook for an additional 5-7 minutes.
4. Serve with rice or bread.

*Chicken Kabob with bell peppers*

## Turkey Kabobs

1 lb. ground turkey
½ onion
¼ cup of oil
2 bell peppers
2-3 tablespoons coriander
½ teaspoon turmeric
½ cup fresh cilantro
2-3 cloves of garlic (minced)
1 teaspoon fresh ginger
Salt
Pepper

1. Put the bell pepper, onion, and cilantro in a food processor and chop finely.
2. Mix well the ground beef and the onion mixture along with the garlic, ginger, salt, pepper, coriander, and turmeric.
3. Make patties with the meat mixture. Brush each patty with oil on both sides.
4. In a skillet, heat the oil. Place the patties in the skillet, cover the skillet, and lower the heat to medium. Allow to cook until the meat has lightly browned and the juices have evaporated. Check frequently to make sure patties are not burning.

## Fire Grilled Chicken Kabob

2 ½ -3 lbs. boneless chicken breasts cut into 1-inch cubes
½ cup oil
2 lemons (juiced)
3 cloves of garlic (minced)
2 teaspoons thyme
1 teaspoon salt

½ teaspoon coarsely ground black pepper
8 cherry tomatoes
1 onion, cut in large chunks
1-2 green bell peppers cut in 1-inch squares

1. Put the chicken cubes in a bowl.
2. Mix together the oil, lemon juice, garlic, thyme, salt, and black pepper.
3. Pour over the chicken and blend well.
4. Refrigerate in a covered container over night.
5. Thread the chicken on the skewers alternately with the cherry tomatoes, onions, and bell peppers.
6. Grill over a charcoal fire, turning and basting frequently. Be careful not to overcook.

## ***Lamb Shish Kabob***

3 lbs. Boneless lamb shoulder or leg, cut into 1-inch cubes
1 medium onion (grated)
1 ½ teaspoon salt
2-3 tablespoons of oil
1 tablespoon vinegar
1 teaspoon coarsely ground pepper
½ teaspoon thyme leaves
1 green bell pepper, cut into 1-inch squares
1 red bell pepper, cut into 1-inch squares
1 large onion, cut in quarters
8-16 cherry Tomatoes

1. Put the meat cubes in a bowl. Mix the grated onion with the meat.
2. Add the olive oil, vinegar, pepper, and thyme to the meat mixture. Mix thoroughly.

3. Cut the bell peppers in large chunks and add on top of the meat mixture.
4. Refrigerate in a covered container over night.
5. Remove the meat from the refrigerator 30 minutes prior to cooking. Mix well.
6. Cut onion in large chunks and set aside.
7. Thread the meat on the skewers alternately with the onion chunks, bell peppers, and tomatoes.
8. Broil over charcoal, turning skewers frequently for about 5-7 minutes. Make sure not to overcook or the meat will be dry and lose its flavor.
9. Serve immediately.

## *Marinated Chicken Kabob*

1 frying chicken or 1 lb. boneless chicken breasts
1-2 cups of yogurt
½ grated onion
3-4 cloves of garlic (minced)
1 lemon (juiced)
1 tablespoon ground cumin
1 tablespoon paprika
Salt (to taste)
Pepper (to taste)
1-2 bell pepper (optional)

1. Cut the chicken into small pieces.
2. Mix together the yogurt, onion, garlic, lemon juice, cumin, paprika, salt, and pepper.
3. Put the chicken in a mixing bowl and pour the marinade over it. Mix to coat the chicken pieces well.
4. Refrigerate overnight or 8-10 hours.
5. Grill the chicken over a charcoal fire, turning and basting frequently.
6. Allow 20-25 minutes cooking time.

7. Slice bell peppers and place on top of the kabob as garnish (optional).
8. Serve hot

*Marinated Chicken Kabob*

Mantu&
Aushak

# Mantu

*This is a popular dish in Afghanistan. Mantu is best described as steamed meat dumpling, similar to Tibetan and Chinese dishes. This dish can be made from scratch or with pasta wraps. If you want to make from scratch, follow the dough recipe for Aushak below.*

## Meat Mixture

1 lb. ground beef or turkey
1 onion
1 bunch of cilantro
½ teaspoon of ground red chili peppers
½ teaspoon ground black pepper
1-2 tablespoon coriander
3-4 cloves of minced garlic
1 cup of water

1. In a food processor, coarsely chop the onion and cilantro.
2. In a pot, add 1 cup of water along with the cilantro, onion, ground meat, garlic, red chili peppers, black pepper, and coriander. Cook for10-15 minutes on medium heat.
3. Set aside.

## Sauce Base

1 medium onion (chopped)
¼ lb. of ground beef or turkey
2-3 tablespoons of oil
2 tablespoons of tomato paste
2-3 tablespoons coriander
1 teaspoon turmeric
1 teaspoon ginger (fresh grated or ground)
1-2 cloves of garlic (minced)

¼ cup dal nakhud (pre-washed and soaked)
Salt
Pepper
1-2 cups of water

1. In a sauce pan, sauté onion in the oil until transparent.
2. Add the beef and stir until browned.
3. Add the tomato paste, garlic, coriander, turmeric, salt, pepper, and ginger along with water. Mix well and cook on low to medium heat.
4. In a separate pot, cook the dal nakhud with 2 cups of water on medium low heat for 10 minutes.
5. Drain the water once the dal nakhud softens and add to the sauce base. Cook an additional 5 minutes on medium low heat.
6. Keep warm and set aside.

**Yogurt mix**

1 cup of yogurt or quroot
2-3 cloves of garlic
Crushed dried mint

1 package of Chinese Pasta Wraps (small squares)

1. Take the pasta wraps and fill them with a small amount of the meat mixture, wet the edges and close, making little triangles.
2. Brush the pasta wraps with a little bit of oil on both sides and set aside until all are filled.
3. In a steam pot, add water on the bottom and grease the steamer with a little bit of oil (this is to prevent the mantu from sticking). Add the mantu to the pot.

4. Cover the pot with a lid and allow to cook on medium heat for about 35-45 minutes. Check the pot occasionally for proper water level for steaming.
5. Smear the 2-3 tablespoons of the yogurt mix on the bottom of a platter.
6. Gently remove the mantu from the steamer and lay on top of the yogurt in the platter.
7. Add the sauce base on top of the mantu and cover with more yogurt mix. Sprinkle red pepper if desired along with crushed dried mint.
8. Serve.

## *Aushak*

*This dish is similar to raviolis but filled with leeks and topped with ground meat sauce and yogurt. Although traditionally this dish requires beef or lamb, I am including turkey meat as a substitute.*

*This dish has several steps to keep in mind but once you get the hang of it, it will not seem so overwhelming. It's best to make the meat sauce in advance. All the hard work will be worth it once you taste how delicious aushak is.*

**Meat Sauce**

1 medium onion (chopped)
¼ lb. of ground beef or turkey
2-3 tablespoons of oil
2 tablespoons of tomato paste
1-2 tablespoon coriander
1 teaspoon turmeric
1 teaspoon ginger (fresh grated or ground)
1-2 cloves of garlic (minced)
¼ cup dal nakhud (pre-washed and soaked)

Salt
Pepper
1-2 cups of water

1. In a sauce pan, sauté onion in the oil until transparent.
2. Add the meat and stir until browned.
3. Add the tomato paste, garlic, coriander, turmeric, salt, pepper, and ginger along with water. Mix well and cook on low to medium heat for 10-15 minutes.
4. In a separate pot, cook the dal nakhud with 2 cups of water on medium low heat for 10 minutes.
5. Drain the water once the dal nakhud softens and add to the sauce base. Cook for an additional 5 minutes on medium low heat.
6. Keep warm and set aside

**Yogurt mix**

1 cup of yogurt or quroot
2-3 cloves of garlic
Crushed dried mint

**Gandana Mix**

1 cup of chopped Gundana (or Chives/leeks)
1 teaspoon dried crushed red peppers
Salt (to taste)

1. Thoroughly wash the Gundana and chop finely.
2. Add salt and crushed red peppers to the Gundana and mix well. Set aside.

***Chinese Pasta Wrappers (small round package)***

1. Take one wrapper out of the package and wet the outer edges with water.

2. Place a small amount of chopped Gundana in the center and close the wrapper, making a semi-circle. Keep doing this until all the Gundana is finished.
3. Fill a large pot ¾ of the way with water and bring to a boil.
4. Add the finished rounds to the boiling water and boil for about 8-10 minutes.
5. In the meantime mix the yogurt with the garlic in a bowl.
6. In a large platter, smear 2 tablespoons of yogurt mix on the platter
7. Gently remove the rounds out of the water, and put the drained pasta rounds on top of the yogurt.
8. Put the meat sauce on the pasta rounds.
9. Put 4-5 tablespoons of yogurt on top of the entire platter.
10. Sprinkle mint over the yogurt and meat sauce and serve.

***Alternative: Dough Mix***

2-3 cups all purpose flour
1 tablespoon oil
1 teaspoon salt
1 teaspoon yeast

1. Add salt and yeast to the flour and mix.
2. Slowly add the water along with the oil to the flour mix and knead the dough real well. Knead until dough becomes smooth.
3. Divide dough in to 2-3 balls, set aside and cover for about an hour.
4. Once dough has risen, take a small chunk out of the balls, make a small ball out of it and roll out on a floured board with a rolling pin. Roll out to a thin round circle.
5. Use a round cutter about 2-3 inches in diameter to cut out rounds. Repeat until dough is finished. Flour rounds and don't place directly on top of each other so they don't stick together.

6. Using the water from the Gundana, or regular water, wet one side of the rounds, on the edge.
7. Take a small amount of Gundana and place in the center of the rounds. Bring edges of rounds together and seal carefully. Set aside until all are done.
8. Fill a large pot ¾ of the way with water and bring to a boil.
9. Add finished rounds to the boiling water and boil for about 8-10 minutes.
10. In the meantime mix the yogurt with the garlic in a bowl.
11. In a large platter, smear 2 tablespoons of yogurt mix on the platter.
12. Gently remove the rounds out of the water, and put the drained pasta rounds on top of the yogurt.
13. Put the meat sauce on the dough rounds.
14. Put 4-5 tablespoons of yogurt on top of the entire platter.
15. Sprinkle mint over the yogurt and meat sauce.
16. Serve.

## ***Shell Pasta with Yogurt sauce***

*Having lived in the United States for 30 years, we've adapted some Western food in our cuisine. Shell pasta with yogurt sauce is one Western dish that has been "Afghanized". My mom popularized this dish by mixing Afghan ingredients with Italian spices. She also steams the pasta and tops with yogurt and gundana for added flavor. This has been a hit at several dinner parties.*

### **Ground Meat Sauce**

1 large onion (chopped)
1 lb. of ground beef or turkey
2-3 tablespoons of oil

2-3 tablespoons of tomato paste
1 tablespoon Italian seasoning
½ can red kidney beans (rinsed and drained)
Salt (to taste)
Pepper (to taste)
¼ cup dal nakhud (pre-washed and soaked)
1 to 2 cloves of garlic (minced)
1-2 cups of water

1. In a sauce pan, heat the oil and sauté the onions until they are transparent.
2. Add the ground meat and stir until browned.
3. Add the water along with the tomato paste, garlic, kidney beans, Italian seasoning, salt, and pepper. Mix well.
4. In a separate pot, cook the dal nakhud with 2 cups of water on medium low heat for 10 minutes.
5. Cover the pot and cook on low to medium heat for 15-20 minutes.
6. Drain the water once the dal nakhud softens and add to the sauce base. Cook for an additional 5 minutes on medium low heat.
7. Keep warm and set aside.

1 package of large shell pasta
1 cup of yogurt
Dried crushed mint or fresh cilantro
½ cup chopped Gundana (or leeks)

1. Prepare the ground meat sauce. Set aside.
2. Boil the pasta shells in water until al dente (not too soft).
3. Drain the pasta and put in a deep dish pot with a lid.
4. Take out 1-2 cups of meat sauce and mix with pasta in the pot. Add ¼ cup of water. Mix well with pasta.
5. Cover the lid with a clean cloth and place on the pot.

6. Steam the pasta on medium low heat for about 10-15 minutes.
7. Remove the pasta and place on a platter.
8. Add an additional cup of meat sauce over the pasta.
9. Sprinkle chopped gundana over the meat sauce and pasta.
10. Add ½ cup of yogurt over the gundana and sprinkle with mint or cilantro.
11. Serve with additional meat sauce and yogurt separately to be added per individual taste.

*Shell Pasta with Yogurt Sauce*

Soups:
Aush,
Maushawa, etc.

*I love Aush on cold rainy days. I typically make a huge pot and eat a little bit over the course of a week. It's filling and deeply satisfying. I love the sauce and yogurt combination. For the vegetarian version of Aush, please refer to the vegetarian soup section on page **156**.*

# Aush with meat

1 package of eggnoodles
8 cups of water
Ground meat sauce
1 tablespoons of crushed mint

## Ground Meat Sauce

1 large onion (chopped)
1 lb. of ground beef or turkey
2-3 tablespoons of oil
2-3 tablespoons of tomato paste
1-2 tablespoon coriander
1 teaspoon turmeric
½ cup of kidney beans
½ cup of chick-peas
Salt (to taste)
Pepper (to taste)
½ teaspoon ginger (fresh grated or ground)
1-2 cloves of garlic (minced)
1-2 cups of water

1. In a sauce pan, heat the oil and sauté the onions until they are transparent.
2. Add the ground meat and stir until browned.
3. Add the water along with the tomato paste, garlic, coriander, turmeric, salt, pepper, and ginger. Mix well.

4. Cover the pot and cook on low to medium heat for 15-20 minutes.
5. Add the chickpeas and beans and cook for an additional 5 minutes.

**Yogurt Mix**

3 cups of yogurt or Quroot
1 clove of garlic (minced)

❖ In a bowel mix 1 clove of garlic to the yogurt or quroot and set aside.

1. In a separate deep pot, bring the water to a boil.
2. Add the noodles with a pinch of salt and boil for 8-10 minutes.
3. Drain the noodles.
4. Put the noodles in big bowl and mix with 3-4 cups of the meat sauce.
5. Add the yogurt mix to the noodles and mix.
6. Sprinkle with mint and serve in bowls.

*Aush*

# *Maushawa (Bean and Meatball Soup)*

Meatball quarma
8 oz. finely ground meat (beef, lamb, or turkey)
½ teaspoon salt
½ cup oil
1 large onion (chopped)
½ teaspoons freshly ground black pepper
¼ teaspoon hot chili pepper
¼ teaspoon ground cinnamon
Water

1. Combine the ground meat with the salt, black pepper, chili pepper, and cinnamon.
2. Shape the meat into small round balls (ping-pong size).
3. Boil 4-5 cups of water in a deep pot.
4. Place the meatballs in the boiling water for 3-4 minutes and then remove from the water and place on a platter.
5. Heat the oil in a large skillet and sauté the onion until transparent and lightly browned.
6. Add the meatballs and sauté on medium low heat with the onions, stirring often, until browned.
7. Stir in 1-2 cups of water and tomatoes to the skillet. Cover and simmer for 30 minutes. This can be done simultaneously while the beans are cooking.

Maushawa:

½ cup dried red kidney beans (washed and soaked overnight)
½ cup dried garbanzo beans (washed and soaked overnight)
Water
½ cup dal nakhud (pre-washed and soaked in advance).
½ cup mung beans
½ cup long grain rice
Salt

½ cup finely chopped cilantro
Water
½ cup chopped tomatoes
1 teaspoon dill (shibit)-dry or fresh
1 cup yogurt

1. Drain the beans and place in a large pot, add 3-4 cups of water and bring to a boil. Cover and simmer on medium low heat for 40 minutes.
2. Wash the dal nakhud and mung beans. Add them to the pot with 2 more cups of water. Allow to simmer for an additional 15-20 minutes.
3. Wash the rice and add to the pot with 2 teaspoons of salt. Simmer for another 30 minutes until the ingredients are soft.
4. Add ¾ of the meatball quarma to the large pot along with 2 additional cups of water.
5. Add the dill and fresh cilantro to the pot and mix.
6. Bring the pot to a boil and cook for an additional 5-7 minutes.
7. Add the yogurt, stirring over low heat until almost boiling.
8. Adjust seasoning with salt and more chili pepper if desired.
9. Serve hot in bowls.
10. Place an additional spoonful of meatball quarma over the Maushawa and sprinkle crushed dried mint over bowls if desired.

## *Vegetable Soup with Chicken, Beef, or Lamb*

1 lb. of chicken, beef, or lamb
2-3 tablespoons of oil
1 onion (chopped)
Salt (to taste)
1 cup of cilantro (washed and chopped)

Black pepper (to taste)
1-2 tablespoons coriander
1 teaspoon turmeric
1 teaspoon ginger (fresh grated or ground)
1 bag of frozen vegetable mix
2 potatoes (peeled and cut in quarters)
½ can of garbanzo beans
½ can of kidney beans
2 cloves of garlic (minced)
8-12 cups of water

1. For beef and lamb meat, wash the meat clean and place in a deep pot and add water.
2. Boil the meat in the water for 5-7 minutes. Remove the meat from the water.
3. In a deep soup pot heat the oil, and sauté the onion until transparent.
4. For chicken: Clean the chicken, rinse, and add to the onions.
5. For beef and lamb: Transfer the meat to the onion mixture and stir for 2-3 minutes.
6. Fill the pot ½ way with water and allow to boil for 10 minutes.
7. Add the potatoes, frozen vegetable mix, garbanzo beans, kidney beans, garlic, turmeric, coriander, ginger, salt, and pepper.
8. Mix in the tomato paste and stir. Add an additional 4-5 cups of water as needed.
9. Cover the pot and allow to cook on medium heat for 15-20 minutes.
10. Add the chopped cilantro and cook for an additional 5 minutes.

## Bean Soup (7 bean mix)

*This is my favorite soup when I'm feeling under the weather. It has all the ingredients necessary to boost my immune system and put me back on track. The onions and garlic along with the chicken and cilantro help me feel better in no time.*

*The 7-bean mix is commonly found in bulk in most health food stores. Beans should be washed and soaked ahead of time, preferably over an hour.*

1 pound of chicken, beef, or lamb
2-3 tablespoons of oil
¼ cup of 7 bean mix (dry) (washed and soaked in advance)
1 large onion (sliced)
2 potatoes (cut in quarters)
1 cup of frozen vegetable mix
¼ cup of frozen green peas
3-4 cloves of garlic (minced)
2-3 tablespoons of tomato paste
1-2 tablespoon coriander
1 teaspoon ginger (fresh grated or ground)
Salt (to taste)
Pepper (to taste)
1 lemon or lime
Water
Fresh cilantro

1. Wash the meat thoroughly and cut into chunks.
2. In a deep soup pot, heat the oil and sauté the onions until transparent.
3. Add the meat to sautéed onions and stir onion, oil and meat together.

4. Add 5-6 cups of water along with bean mix. Cover the pot and cook for 20-25 minutes.
5. Add the potatoes and 2-3 cups of more water as needed. Boil for an additional 5-7 minutes.
6. Add the frozen vegetable mix, peas, tomato paste, garlic, salt, pepper, ginger, turmeric, and coriander. Mix well and boil for an additional 5-10 minutes.
7. Add the fresh cilantro and cook for additional 3-5 minutes.
8. Once ready, put in bowls and serve with lemon and bread. The lemon juice makes it more flavorful and adds vitamin C.

Vegetarian
Soups

# Bean and Vegetable Soup

2-3 tablespoons of oil
¼ cup of 7 bean mix (dry) (washed and soaked in advance)
1 large onion (sliced)
2 potatoes (cut in quarters)
1 cup of frozen mixed "Fiesta" Vegetable mix
10-15 spaghetti noodles (broken into 4 quarters)
¼ cup of frozen green peas
3-4 cloves of garlic (minced)
2-3 tablespoons of tomato paste
1-2 tablespoon coriander
1 teaspoon ginger (fresh grated or ground)
Fresh cilantro
Salt (to taste)
Pepper (to taste)
1 lemon or lime
Water

1. In a deep soup pot heat, the oil and sauté the onions until transparent.
2. Add 4-5 cups of water along with bean mix and cook for 20-25 minutes.
3. Add the potatoes and 2-3 cups of more water as needed. Boil for an additional 5-7 minutes.
4. Add the frozen vegetable mix, peas, spaghetti noodles, tomato paste, garlic, salt, pepper, ginger, turmeric, and coriander. Mix well and boil for an additional 5-10 minutes.
5. Add the fresh cilantro and cook for additional 3-5 minutes.
6. Once ready, put in bowls and serve with lemon and bread. The lemon juice makes it more flavorful.

- *The 7-bean mix is commonly found in bulk in most health food stores. Beans should be washed and soaked ahead of time, preferably over an hour.*

## Aush

*This recipe was kindly shared by my cousin Malalai.*

1 package of Chinese egg noodles
1-2 potatoes (chopped in small chunks)
1 can of garbanzo beans (drained and rinsed)
1 ½ can of kidney beans (drained and rinsed)
3-4 quarts of water
1 cup tomato sauce
3 tablespoons of oil
Red pepper (ground or crushed)
2 cloves of garlic (minced)
1-2 tablespoon coriander
½ teaspoon turmeric
½ teaspoon black pepper
Salt
1-2 cups of yogurt
Crushed dried mint

1. In a colander, rinse the kidney and garbanzo beans. Separate half a can of kidney beans and set aside.
2. In a saucepan, heat the oil and add the tomato sauce, garlic, coriander, turmeric, peppers, salt, and ½ can of kidney beans. Simmer for 10 minutes on medium low heat.
3. In a deep pot bring the water to a boil and add the potatoes. Cover the pot and cook for 5-8 minutes.
4. Add the noodles along with 1 tablespoon of salt. Allow to cook for 10-15 minutes on medium high heat.

5. Add the kidney beans and garbanzo beans to the noodles and mix. Cook for an additional 1-2 minutes.
6. Using a ladle, transfer the Aush from the pot to a deep soup serving dish. Mix in 1 cup of yogurt.
7. Add the sauce to the Aush and mix.
8. Sprinkle mint and red pepper as desired and serve in bowls.

## ***Aush: Alternative Version***

½ package of egg-noodles
8 cups of water
2-3 tablespoons of oil
1 onion (sliced)
2-3 tablespoons of tomato paste
2 cloves of garlic (minced)
3 cups of plain yogurt
1 can of kidney beans (rinse)
1 can of garbanzo beans (rinse)
1-2 potatoes
Salt (to taste)
Pepper (to taste)
1-2 tablespoon coriander
1 teaspoon turmeric
1 teaspoon ginger (fresh grated or ground)
1 tablespoon of crushed dry mint

1. In a deep pot, sauté the onions in oil until golden brown.
2. Peel and cut the potatoes in quarters then add to the onions along with 2 cups of water. Boil for 5-7 minutes.
3. Add the noodles, tomato paste, salt, kidney beans, garbanzo beans, pepper, minced garlic, coriander, turmeric, and ginger along with 5-6 cups of water.
4. Cover the pot and allow to boil for 20 minutes on medium heat.

5. Transfer the Aush to a deep bowl and mix in the yogurt.
6. Sprinkle crushed dry mint over the Aush and serve.

# Lemon & Potato Soup

4-5 carrots (peeled and sliced)
2-3 tablespoons of oil
1 onion (sliced)
2-3 large potatoes
3-4 lemons (juiced)
1 teaspoon turmeric
1 teaspoon ginger (fresh grated or ground)
1 tablespoon coriander
4-5 cloves of garlic (minced)
Salt (to taste)
Black pepper (to taste)
8-10 cups of water

1. In a deep pot, heat up the oil and sauté the onion until golden brown.
2. Add the carrots along with 2-3 cups of water. Cover the pot and allow to cook for 8-10 minutes.
3. Peel and cut the potatoes in quarters and add to the pot. Add 5-6 cups of water to the pot. Cover the pot and cook for 15-20 minutes.
4. Add the lemon juice, salt, pepper, turmeric, ginger, coriander, and garlic. Allow to cook for an additional 5-10 minutes.
5. Once the carrots and potatoes are cooked, use a hand held blender and puree the vegetables in the pot, making sure all the vegetables are pureed and mixed.
6. Serve in bowls with warm toasted Afghan bread.

# Butternut Squash Soup

*I love this soup. I used to buy it ready made in a box but realized the homemade version is so much tastier and healthier.*

1 Butternut squash (peeled and cubed)
4-5 carrots (peeled and sliced)
2-3 tablespoons of oil
1 onion (sliced)
2-3 large potatoes
1 teaspoon turmeric
1 teaspoon ginger (fresh grated or ground)
1 tablespoon coriander
4-5 cloves of garlic (minced)
Salt (to taste)
Black pepper (to taste)
8-10 cups of water

1. In a deep pot, heat up the oil and sauté the onion until golden brown.
2. Add the carrots and butternut squash cubes along with 4-5 cups of water. Cover the pot and allow to cook for 8-10 minutes on medium heat.
3. Peel and cut the potatoes in quarters and add to the pot. Add 6-8 cups of water to the pot. Cover the pot and cook for 15-20 minutes.
4. Add the salt, pepper, turmeric, ginger, coriander, and garlic. Allow to cook for an additional 5-10 minutes.
5. Once the vegetables are cooked, use a hand held blender and puree the vegetables in the pot, making sure all the vegetables are pureed and mixed.
6. Serve in bowls with warm toasted Afghan bread.

# ***Carrot & Ginger Soup***

4-5 carrots (peeled and sliced)
2-3 tablespoons of oil
1 onion (sliced)
2-3 large potatoes
1 teaspoon turmeric
2-3 tablespoon fresh grated ginger
1 tablespoon coriander
4-5 cloves of garlic (minced)
Salt (to taste)
Black pepper (to taste)
1 cup chopped cilantro
8-10 cups of water

1. In a deep pot, heat up the oil and sauté the onion until golden brown.
2. Add the carrots along with 4-5 cups of water. Cover the pot and allow to cook for 8-10 minutes.
3. Peel and cut the potatoes in quarters and add to the pot. Add 6-8 cups of water to the pot. Cover the pot and cook for 15-20 minutes.
4. Add the salt, pepper, turmeric, ginger, coriander, cilantro, and garlic. Allow to cook for an additional 5-10 minutes.
5. Once the vegetables are cooked, use a hand held blender and puree the vegetables in the pot, making sure all the vegetables are pureed and mixed.
6. Serve in bowls with warm toasted Afghan bread.

Dolmas

# Dolma (Base)

½ pound of ground beef
1 medium onion
2-3 tablespoons of oil
1 cup of Birinj-e-luk (long grain rice)
2 tablespoons of tomato puree
1 clove of garlic (minced)
1 teaspoon of ginger (fresh grated or ground)
Salt (to taste)
Pepper (to taste)

1. Dice the onions and sauté in oil until golden brown.
2. Add ground beef and garlic and stir with onions and oil until browned.
3. Add tomato, salt, pepper, and ginger and stir.
4. In a separate pot bring the rice to a boil until slightly soft.
5. Drain the water and add to the beef pot.

***Sauce***
1 medium onion
3-4 tablespoons of oil
1 cup water
1 clove of garlic (minced)
½ cup tomato puree
1 teaspoon of turmeric
3-4 fresh jalapeno peppers
Salt (to taste)
Pepper (to taste)

1. Dice onions and sauté in oil until golden brown.
2. Add tomato puree, garlic, turmeric, jalapeno peppers and water and let boil for 5 minutes.

# Dolma Banjan (Eggplant)

3 medium eggplants
½ pound of ground beef
1 medium onion
4 tablespoons of oil
1 cup of Birinj-e-luk (long grain rice)
2 tablespoons of tomato puree
1 clove of garlic
1 teaspoon of ginger (fresh grated or ground)
Salt (to taste)
Pepper (to taste)

1. Dice onions and sauté in oil until golden brown.
2. Add ground beef and garlic and stir with onions and oil until browned.
3. Add tomato, salt, pepper, and ginger and stir.
4. In a separate pot bring rice to a boil until slightly soft.
5. Drain the water and add to the beef pot.
6. Wash the eggplant, cut the top and set aside.
7. Dig out the meat of the eggplant and fill with dolma.
8. Fill all three and put the top back on the eggplant.
9. Place eggplants close together in a deep pot.
10. Add sauce over the eggplants and cover the pot.
11. Let cook on low for 20-25 minutes.

# Dolma Murch Shireen (Bell Peppers)

3-5 Bell peppers
½ pound of ground beef
1 medium onion
4 tablespoons of oil
1 cup of Birinj-e-luk (long grain rice)
2 tablespoons of tomato puree
1 clove of garlic
1 teaspoon of ginger (fresh grated or ground)
Salt (to taste)

Pepper (to taste)

1. Dice onions and sauté in oil until golden brown.
2. Add ground beef and garlic and stir with onions and oil until browned.
3. Add tomato, salt, pepper, and ginger and stir.
4. In a separate pot bring rice to a boil until slightly soft.
5. Drain water and add to the beef pot.
6. Wash bell peppers, cut the top and set aside.
7. Dig out the seeds of the peppers and fill with dolma.
8. Fill all and put the top back on the peppers.
9. Place peppers close together in a deep pot.
10. Add sauce over the peppers and cover the pot.
11. Let cook on low for 20-25 minutes.

## ***Dolma Banjan Rumi (Tomatoes)***

4-5 Large Tomatoes
½ pound of ground beef
1 medium onion
4 tablespoons of oil
1 cup of Birinj-e-luk (long grain rice)
2 tablespoons of tomato puree
1 clove of garlic
1 teaspoon of ginger (fresh grated or ground)
Salt (to taste)
Pepper (to taste)

1. Dice onions and sauté in oil until golden brown.
2. Add ground beef and garlic and stir with onions and oil until browned.
3. Add tomato, salt, pepper, and ginger and stir.
4. In a separate pot bring rice to a boil until slightly soft.
5. Drain water and add to the beef pot.
6. Wash the tomatoes, cut the top and set aside.

7. Dig out the meat of the tomatoes and fill with dolma.
8. Fill all and put the top back on the tomatoes.
9. Place the tomatoes close together in a deep pot.
10. Add sauce over the tomatoes and cover the pot.
11. Let cook on low for 20-25 minutes.

Bread&
Desserts

# Jillabee

*This recipe was kindly given to me by my aunt "Maggie" (Khala Magul). She's the expert Jillabee maker in the family. Jillabee's are delicious desserts that are very sweet and best with tea. The first time I made this, I messed up the syrup and it became too hard and the jillabee stuck together and became hard like rock candy. If you boil the syrup for about 8 minutes and then allow to cool, you can tell the consistency more accurately and adjust it as needed.*

1 cup all purpose flour
1 leveled teaspoon dry yeast
8-10 drops of yellow food coloring
1 cup of water
Oil for frying

1. In a bowl, mix the flour, yeast, food coloring and water. Use a whisk to mix together for about 1-2 minutes.
2. Cover the bowl and allow to sit for about 15-30 minutes. After 15 minutes, the mixture should be bubbling.
3. Add the mixture to a refillable condiment bottle (squeezable empty and unused ketchup/mustard bottle) and set aside.

**Sugar Base**
½ lemon juice
2 ½ cups of sugar
2 cups of water
8-10 drops of yellow food coloring

1. In a saucepan, add sugar and water and allow to boil for about 8-10 minutes.
2. Add ½ lemon juice and mix. Allow to boil for an additional 1-2 minutes.
3. Add 1-2 drops of yellow food coloring and mix.
4. Allow the syrup to cool. (At this point the syrup should not be too runny and not too thick. If it is too runny, add ½ cup additional sugar and bring to a boil again and if too thick, add ½ cup of water and boil for 2-3 minutes.) Set syrup aside to cool.

**Making the Jillabee**

1. In a deep-set frying pan, add 4-5 cups of oil and heat on high. Once oil is heated, lower the heat to medium high.
2. Take the flour mixture and squeeze circular shapes (similar to making a pretzel) in the oil and allow to fry for 1-2 minutes. Dip with a fork to ensure both sides are fried.
3. Remove from the oil and dip into the sugar mixture for about 1 minute. *(Important Note: Use a separate fork for the sugar and oil. If the sugar fork touches the oil, it will darken the oil and ruin the jillabee).*
4. Remove the jillabee from the sugar mixture and set on a platter. Follow the same procedure for the additional mixture until finished.
5. Place the jillabee on a platter. Do not set them directly on top of each other.
6. Serve with tea.

# Khajour

*This is the specialty of my aunts Aquila and Zareen. Khajour is a very delicious desert that is great with tea.*

6 eggs
1 cup "Jiffy" baking mix
1 ½ cups of sugar
4 cups of all purpose flour (or "Elephant Brand" Wheat flour found in most Indian stores)
1 cup of milk
¼ to ½ cup of oil
1 tablespoon of cardamom
1 teaspoon dry yeast
1 tablespoon baking powder
Oil for frying

1. Mix the sugar, eggs, milk, oil, and cardamom in a bowl.
2. Add the flour, yeast, baking powder, and Jiffy baking mix to the bowl and mix well.
3. Knead the dough until it becomes elastic. Allow to sit covered for 20-30 minutes (it can sit for up to 10 hours if needed).
4. Take a piece of the mixture (about the size of a walnut) and roll in your hands and then shape into small rolls.
5. Using a mesh colander or a mesh strainer, press the roll against the mesh and take your thumb to press in the center to create an indent. Do the same for the rest of mixture.
6. In a skillet, heat 3-4 cups of oil and fry the Khajour on medium low heat until browned.
7. Place on a cake rack to drain the oil or use a paper towel to absorb the oil on a platter.
8. Serve with tea.

Khajour

## Mehwa-e-Tarkada (Dried Fruit drink)

*This is a drink made especially for the Afghan New Year's. Since New Year's day is the 1st day of Spring, this drink is analogous to Spring (dried fruit comes back to life after being soaked in water). I look forward to making this drink every Spring as part of my ritual of welcoming Spring back. The drink is very delicious as well as nutritious.*

1 lb. of almonds
1 lb. of walnuts
1 package of sinjit (oleaster)*
½ lb. of black raisins
½ lb. of green raisins
½ lb. of dried apricots
3-4 quarts of water
*Found in Afghan Stores

1. In 2 separate bowls, add the almonds and the walnuts. Boil enough water to cover the nuts. Pour the hot boiling water over the nuts, cover the bowls, and allow to soak for 1-2 days on the countertop or in the refrigerator.
2. In a separate large bowl, add the raisins, Sinjit, and the apricots. Add 3-4 quarts of boiling filtered water over the dried fruit and allow to soak for 1-2 days in the refrigerator.
3. After 1-2 days, drain the water from the bowl of almonds. Peel the almonds.
4. After peeling the almonds, mix the almonds with the other fruit mixture. The mix should be soupy by this time and the juice very sweet.
5. You can either peel the walnuts and add to the mix or leave the unpeeled walnuts separate from the mix until ready to serve (the unpeeled walnuts darken the rest of the ingredients if left in to soak so it's best to keep it separate until ready to serve.
6. At the time of serving, add a few spoonfuls of walnuts to the fruit mixture and serve in a cup or bowl with a spoon.

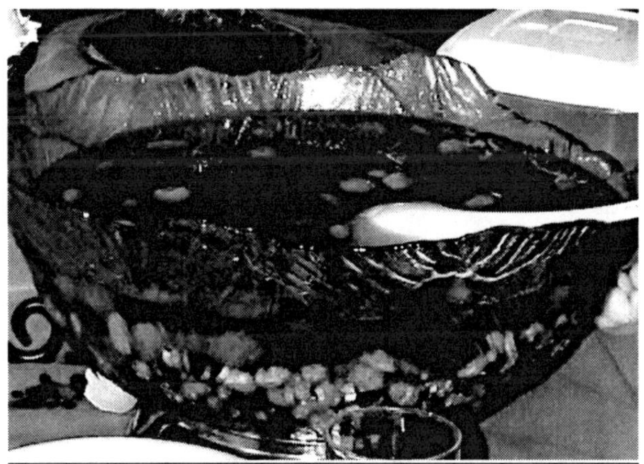

*Mewah Tarkada*

# Samanac

*This is a dish made especially during the Afghan New Year. In Afghanistan, making samanac was an all day event and a social occasion for families. They would bring food, build an outside fire pit, place a very large pot on the fire, and take turns stirring the pot for hours as they socialized over food and tea. At the end of the day, all would share in the reward by distributing the samanac among all the participants. So invite some friends over, make some food and tea, and start taking turns stirring the pot! It will be a tradition you'll want to continue for years.*

*The traditional process of making samanac begins several weeks prior to the preparation if growing your own wheat grass. You can also buy wheat grass from the grocery store these days and avoid the advanced preparation.*

***To grow your own wheat grass in advance:***

1. Take a plastic colander type bowl with holes and place a thin cloth on the bottom.

2. Sprinkle ½ cup of wheat seeds on the cloth and pour water on the seeds.
3. Cover the seeds with a thin cloth and leave outside to grow. Water regularly to prevent seeds from drying.
4. When the grass begins to grow, it will push the cloth up and the roots will grow through the bottom cloth. To remove the grass, simply pull the cloth from the roots prior to grinding.

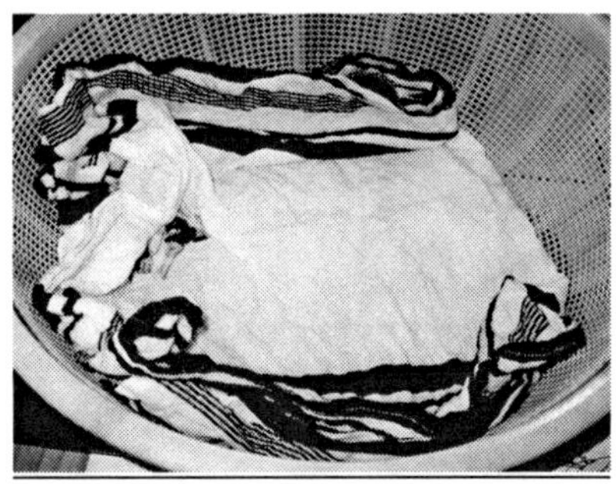

*Step 1*

*Final step*

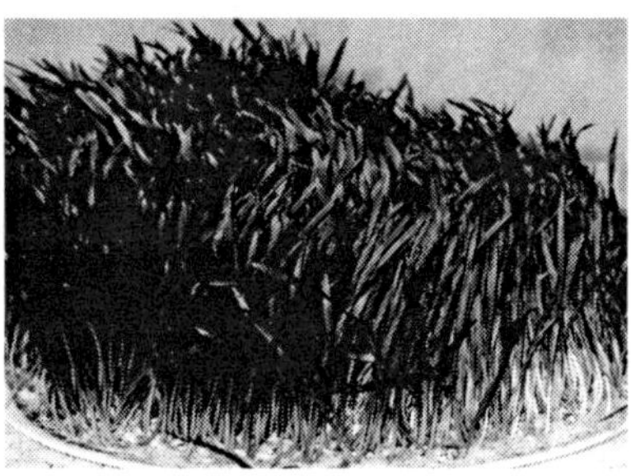

***Ingredients needed:***
1-2 containers of wheat grass
3-4 cups whole wheat flour
1-3 tablespoons white poppy seeds
4-8 whole walnuts in the shells

1. For store bought containers, remove the wheat grass from the containers and thoroughly wash the roots and grass. Remove all the dirt (growing your own wheat grass does not include dirt).
2. Using a *meat grinder (electric meat grinders work best), grind the roots and grass. Capture the juice and pulp in a large bowl.
3. Separate the juice from the pulp using a tight mesh colander or sieve.
4. Take the pulp and add water to it. Squeeze the juice out of the pulp. Keep adding water and squeezing the pulp until all the juice has been squeezed out of the pulp (about 3 times).
5. In a very large and deep pot, add the juice along with 3 ½ cups of whole wheat flour.
6. Use a whisk to mix the flour and juice. If the mixture is too thick, add 1-2 cups of water.
7. Stir constantly to avoid the mixture from separating and burning.
8. Monitor the mix and prevent it from boiling over by constantly stirring it.
9. Reduce the heat to medium high and continue to stir the boiling mixture for about an hour.
10. Reduce the heat to medium, add the whole walnuts, and continue stirring for about 9 hours. Add water if the mixture becomes too thick and continue to stir.
    {Be prepared for the bubbling mixture to make a mess. I'm sure this was traditionally cooked outside for this reason.}
11. Once the mixture has thickened and turned brown, it's ready. The mixture should be fluid...meaning not too

thick and can slide from the spoon. If the mixture is too thick, add more water and cook for an additional 5-10 minutes.

12. To serve, take out the samanac and put in bowls and sprinkle the poppy seeds on top.

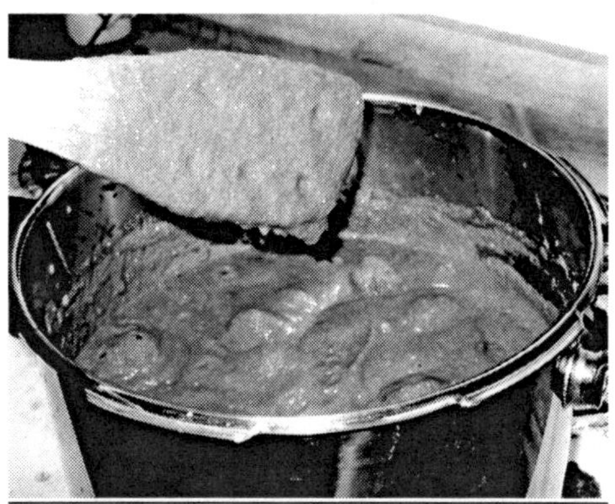

Samanac in liquid reduction stage

*Using a juicer seems to make more sense but it was not effective in getting all the juice out and the majority of the grass was discarded. The meat grinder gets all the juice out and the pulp can then be used to extract more juice.

## ***Halwa e-Aurd***

1 cup oil
½ cup wheat flour
1 cup all purpose flour
1 ½-2 cups of sugar
1 ½ cup hot water
1 teaspoon cardamom
1 teaspoon rosewater (optional)

1. In a 4 quart pot, add 1 cup oil to ½ cup wheat flour and stir to brown on medium heat.
2. Add ½ cup of all-purpose flour and stir until well mixed. Add additional ½ cup and stir.
3. Add sugar slowly (adjust amount as needed) and stir constantly for 10-15 minutes on medium low heat until flour becomes golden brown. Mix well.
4. Slowly add the hot water and stir for 1 minute.
5. Add the cardamom and rose water and stir. Mix well and then wrap the lid in a clean cloth and place on the pot. Cook on low for ½ hour.
6. Remove from heat and serve with pita or afghan bread.

## ***Sheer Birinj***

1 cup long grain rice (Birinj-e-luk)
8-10 cups of water
2-2 ½ cups of milk
2 cups of sugar
½ teaspoon of cardamom
1 tablespoon of rosewater

1. Thoroughly the wash rice and soak for at least an hour.
2. In a deep pot add water and bring to a boil.
3. Drain the water from the rice and put the rice in the boiling water. Cook the rice on medium low heat for about 40-50 minutes or until the rice kernels are really soft.
4. Lower the heat to low, add the milk and sugar, and stir constantly.
5. Add rosewater and cardamom and boil for another 1-2 minutes. Stir constantly to make sure the bottom of the pot doesn't stick. The consistency should not be too runny or too thick.
6. Once the sheer birinj is cooked, take it out of the pot and place in glass containers. Set aside to cool.
7. Once cool, serve with tea.

# Firnee

4 cups of milk
1 cup sugar
½ cup cornstarch
½ cup slivered almonds (optional)
½ to 1 teaspoon ground cardamom
¼ teaspoon saffron threads (optional)
¼ cup finely chopped pistachio nuts (optional)
2 teaspoons of rosewater

1. Put all but ½ cup of milk into a medium size sauce pan.
2. Take the remaining ½ cup of milk and mix with ½ cup of cornstarch.
3. Add the milk and cornstarch mix into the pan with the rest of the milk.
4. Over medium heat, stir the mixture constantly until mixture begins to thicken (about 10-15 minutes).
5. (Optional) Add almonds and keep stirring until mixture thickens and bubbles. Use a whisk if mixture becomes lumpy.
6. Add cardamom and rosewater and stir. Cook on low heat for 10 minutes, allowing the firnee to simmer gently. Stir occasionally.
7. Pour into platter, spreading evenly. Sprinkle pistachio nuts and cardamom on top and around the edge of the firnee.

*Firnee*

## Rhote

2 cups all purpose flour
1 cup wheat flour
½ cup of oil
2 eggs
1 cup milk
1 cup sugar
1 teaspoon ground cardamom
2 teaspoons baking powder
1 tablespoon black caraway seeds
1 tablespoon sesame seeds
1 cup raisins (optional)
Rose water (optional

1. Mix the flour, oil, eggs, sugar, cardamom, raisins (optional), and baking powder.
2. Heat the milk (20-30 seconds in the microwave or 1-2 minutes on the stovetop). Add the heated milk to the flour mixture.

3. Mix all the ingredients and allow to sit in a warm place for 1 hour.
4. Preheat the oven to 350°.
5. Spread the mixture on a cookie sheet.
6. Brush 1 teaspoon of oil and ½ teaspoon of milk over the dough.
7. Sprinkle sia dana (black caraway seeds) and sesame seeds on top.
8. Bake until golden brown (about 20-30 minutes).
9. Remove from the oven, cut into diamond shapes, and serve.

*Rhote*

## Kulcha-e-Khatayee (Almond cookies)

*The recipe for these cookies was kindly given to me by my aunt Faiza and uncle Hafiz. I first tasted these cookies while visiting with my cousin Harrier and instantly fell in love with the taste. The texture of the cookies is dry and crumbly but the taste is delicious.*

5 cups all purpose flour
2 ½ cups sugar
2 cups oil
1 cup dry milk
½ teaspoon baking soda
1 teaspoon cardamom
1 cup whole almonds
3-4 tablespoons of water (as needed)

1. In a deep bowl, mix the flour, oil, sugar, cardamom, baking soda, and dry milk. Use an electric mixer to really mix the dough well.
2. Knead the dough with your hands really well until all the ingredients are soft and well mixed. If needed, add 1-2 tablespoons of water and mix well.
3. Cover the bowl with a towel or plate and allow to sit for 15-20 minutes.
4. Preheat the oven to 350°.
5. Take out a small piece of dough and make walnut size balls. Do this with all the dough.
6. Press your thumb in the center of each ball while holding the ball in your hands, supporting the sides of the ball.
7. Place one almond in the center of the ball and place the ball in a flat cookie sheet. Continue this process with the rest of the dough balls.
8. Place the cookie sheet in the oven for 8-10 minutes. *(If left in the oven too long the cookies will become hard).
9. After 10 minutes, take out the cookies from the oven and allow to cool for 10-15 minutes.
10. Serve with tea.

## ***Baklava with Nuts***

2 cups almonds, walnuts, pistachios
3 tablespoons sugar
1 cup (2 sticks) sweet, unsalted butter
1 lb. thin phyllo pastry

***Syrup***:
1 ¾ cups of sugar
1 ½ cups of water
1 teaspoon lemon juice
2-3 tablespoons rose water (optional)

1. Make the syrup by mixing the water with the 1 ½ cups of sugar and bringing it to a boil. Simmer on medium low heat for 5 minutes.
2. Add the lemon juice and simmer for an additional 5-7 minutes.
3. Cool and add the rose water (optional).

1. Preheat the oven to 350° and butter the baking dish.
2. Coarsely grind the nuts in a spice grinder or food processor.
3. Place the nuts in a mixing bowl and toss with 3 tablespoons of sugar until well blended.
4. Melt the butter.
5. Unfold the phyllo pastry. Take only one sheet at a time and keep the remaining sheets well covered at all times in order to prevent them from drying out.
6. Place half of one sheet on the bottom of the baking dish and leave the other half draped over the side of the pan. Using a pastry brush, brush the half of the sheet on the pan with butter. Fold the other half of the pastry sheet over the first half; brush it with butter. Repeat this process of layering and buttering the pastry sheets until 7 pastry sheets have been used.
7. Spread 1/3 of the nut mixture evenly over the sheets in the pan.
8. Layer another half sheet of phyllo, brush with butter, and spread another 1/3 of the nut mixture on top.
9. Fold the other half of the sheet, brush it with butter, and spread the remaining nuts over it. Continue layering and buttering the sheets until all the phyllo has been used up.
10. Pour the remaining butter over the top. Press the sheets down gently with your hands or the back of a flat spatula.
11. Using a very sharp knife cut the baklava into diagonal strips to form diamond shapes.
12. Bake for 30 minutes at 350°.

13. Reduce the temperature to 300°, place a sheet of aluminum foil loosely over the baklava, and bake for an additional 25 minutes.
14. Remove the baklava from the oven. Tilt the pan and drain off the excess butter.
15. Pour the syrup over the baklava. Allow the baklava to sit for 1-2 hours to fully absorb the syrup.
16. Serve with tea.

## *Chocolate Baklava*

*The chocolate baklava is a delicious alternative to the traditional baklava.*

***Filling:***

½ cups miniature chocolate chips
1 ½ tablespoons ground cinnamon
½ teaspoon ground cloves
2 ½ tablespoons unsweetened cocoa powder
3 tablespoons butter (melted)
2 cups almonds (slivered and coarsely chopped)
2 cups walnuts (coarsely chopped)
¼ teaspoon salt

1. In a food processor coarsely chop the walnuts and almonds.
2. In a bowl, mix together the almonds, walnuts, chocolate chips, cinnamon, cloves, cocoa powder, 3 tablespoons melted butter, and salt. Set aside.

***Syrup:***

2 cups of water
2 cups of sugar
3 strips of lemon zest
1 cinnamon stick
¼ cup whole cloves
½ teaspoon lemon juice
¾ cup honey
1 cup butter (melted)
1/3 cup water

1. In a 2 quart saucepan, mix the water, sugar, lemon zest, and cinnamon stick and bring to a boil over high heat. Boil for about 8 minutes or until the mixture thickens to a syrup consistency. Turn off the heat.
2. Remove the zest and the cinnamon from the syrup.
3. Stir in the lemon juice and honey. Set syrup aside.

***Baklava:***
1 package of phyllo pastry

1. Preheat the oven to 350°.
2. Brush a baking pan with some melted butter and lay one sheet of phyllo pastry into the bottom and up the sides of the pan.
3. Brush the phyllo with melted butter and lay a second sheet of phyllo on top. Continue the brushing and layering process until there are 12 layers of buttered pastry. Spread half of the filling over the pastry layers. Smooth the filling evenly, then press it down firmly.
4. Top the filling with 5 more sheets of pastry, brushing each with butter as it is layered.
5. Spread the remaining half of the filling over the pastry, smooth it evenly, and press it down firmly.

6. Top the filling with 12 more sheets of phyllo, brushing each with butter as it is layered.
7. Cut any excess phyllo from the sides of the baking pan and make sure the top of the baklava is flat.
8. Using a knife, cut the baklava into diamond shapes.
9. Place a single clove in the middle of each diamond shape and sprinkle some water over the top.
10. Place the baklava in the oven and bake for about 1 hour, or until the pastry is crisp and a rich golden color.
11. Remove the baklava from the oven and pour the syrup evenly over the entire surface of the baklava.
12. Allow the baklava to sit for 1-2 hours to fully absorb the syrup.
13. Serve the baklava at room temperature.

*Chocolate Baklava*

# Goush-e-feel (Elephant ears)

*This has been a favorite desert of mine from childhood but when I buy it from the Afghan stores, it never tastes as good as homemade. The first time I made goush-e-feel I ate half the batch the first night. The combination of sugar, nuts, and cardamom is irresistible. My elephant ears are not exactly true to form, but I don't think that's as important as how wonderful this pastry tastes.*

2 eggs
2 teaspoons sugar
¼ teaspoon salt
½ cup milk
4 teaspoons oil
3 cups all purpose flour
Oil for deep frying

**Topping**
1 cup confectioner's sugar
½ teaspoon ground cardamom
½ cup pistachio nuts (ground in advance)

1. In a deep bowl, beat the eggs until frothy.
2. Beat in the sugar and salt with the eggs.
3. Stir in the milk and oil to the eggs.
4. Slowly add 1 cup of flour to the egg mixture and blend in with a wooden spoon. Gradually stir in another 1 ½ cups of flour to the egg mixture. Blend well.
5. Sprinkle flour on a cutting board before putting the dough mixture.
6. Knead the dough for 10 minutes until smooth, using more flour as needed. Dough should be slightly sticky.

7. Cover the dough with a clean cloth or plastic wrap and allow to sit for about 2 hours.
8. Take a piece of dough about the size of a walnut and roll out on a floured board to a circle about 3-4 inches in diameter (can use a circular cutter if desired to get the perfect circular shape but it's not necessary).
9. Gather up the rolled out dough on one side and pinch, forming a shape resembling an elephant ear. Place on a cloth and cover. Repeat with the remaining dough.
10. Heat 2-3 cups of oil in a deep skillet or frying pan. Fry one at a time, turning to cook evenly. Fry until very light golden brown.
11. If the pastry contracts prior to frying, simply pull out slightly.
12. Drain the oil from the pastries on paper towels.
13. Sift the sugar and dust the pastries.
14. Mix the cardamom and ground pistachio nuts together and sprinkle over the pastries.
15. Serve with tea.

*Goush e-Feel*

# Afghan Bread

*When we were new immigrants to the United States, my mom and aunts made Afghan bread weekly. At the time they didn't have the luxury of using a Kitchen Aide mixer to knead the dough, so the process was physically draining. Thankfully today Afghan bread or the dough to make the bread is readily available in most Afghan grocery stores that sell bread. If you don't live near an Afghan grocery store, you can make your own bread using the recipe below.*

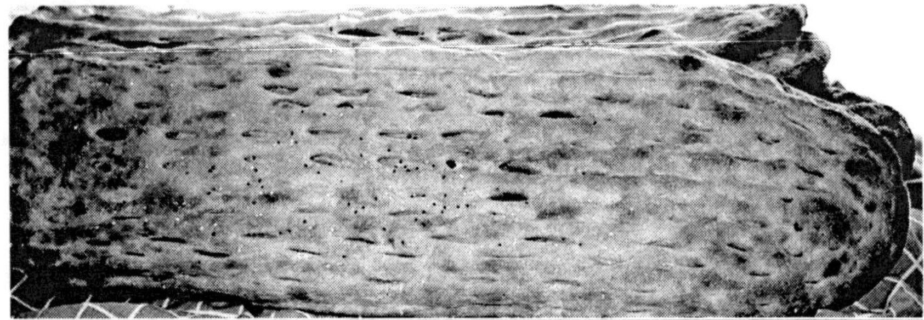

*Afghan Bread*

5-7 cups of warm water
5 cups all purpose flour
2 cups of whole wheat flour
½-1 tablespoons of salt
1 packets of dry yeast
1 tablespoon sugar
½ cup of vegetable oil
1-2 tablespoons sesame seeds (optional)
1-2 tablespoons sia dana (caraway seeds) (optional)
3-4 cookie sheet pans

1. In a large bowl or mixer, mix the wheat flour to the all purpose flour along with the salt, dry yeast, sugar, and oil.
2. Add the water gradually while kneading the dough until the dough is soft yet firm in consistency. Knead dough for 15 minutes consistently.
3. Leave kneaded dough covered for 1 hour, or until the dough has risen.
4. Remove the dough from the bowl and make dough balls the size of saucer plates. Cover the dough balls with a towel or plate for 10-15 minutes.
5. Preheat the oven to 500° degrees.
6. Brush some oil on the cookie sheets.
7. Take the dough balls and stretch the dough across the cookie sheet.
8. Using a butter knife, make 4-5 slashes in the stretched dough to release the trapped air when the dough is baking.
9. Sprinkle sesame seeds and /or sia dana and put the cookie sheets in the oven. Bake until the bread is golden brown.
10. Remove the bread from the oven and brush a little bit of oil on top of bread (optional step).
11. Remove the bread from the cookie sheet and put it on an oven rack to cool.
12. Serve the bread warm.

   *To store bread, cut up in small squares and put in plastic storage bags. Bread can be stored in the freezer for several months if wrapped well in freezer bags.

Favorite
Non-Traditional
Desserts

*I wanted to include a section on a few non-traditional Afghan desserts that have become favorites in my family over the years. Although not traditionally Afghan, these desserts have become part of my family's cuisine.*

## Chocolate and Vanilla Swirl Cheesecake

*This is a recipe made famous by my sister Nahid. Initially I was not a fan of cheesecake but this cake made a huge fan out of me.*

***Crust:***
1 ½ cups graham cracker crumbs
¼ cup sugar
3 tablespoons cocoa powder
½ cup butter (melted)

***Filling:***
1 ½ pounds cream cheese
1 cup plus 2 tablespoons sugar
2 tablespoons all purpose flour
3 whole eggs
½ teaspoon vanilla extract
6 ounces semisweet chocolate
½ cup fresh raspberries or strawberries

1. Preheat the oven to 325° degrees.
2. In a bowl, mix the crust ingredients together.
3. Using a wooden spoon, press the crust ingredients firmly into a 10-inch spring form pan and set aside.
4. Using an electric mixer, beat the cream cheese and sugar together until light and fluffy.
5. Add the flour and mix.
6. Slowly beat in the eggs and vanilla.

7. In a double boiler, melt the chocolate on medium low heat and set aside.
8. Pour ¾ of the cheesecake filling over the crust.
9. Add the melted chocolate to the remaining cheesecake filling and mix well.
10. Pour the chocolate filling over the filling in the pan.
11. Using a knife, swirl the chocolate filling into the plain filling to get a marbled effect.
12. Put the pan in the oven and bake for 40 minutes.
13. Turn off the oven, open the door, and leave the cake in the oven for an additional 20 minutes.
14. Remove the cake from the oven and allow to cool.
15. Refrigerate the cake overnight.
16. To cut the cake in neat slices, heat the knife under hot running water prior to cutting. Rinse the knife after each cut.
17. Sprinkle fresh raspberries or strawberries over the cake and serve.
    *If you don't have fresh fruit, you can substitute fruit sauce such as Marionberry or Blueberry.

## ***Chocolate Coffee Cake***

*This is also my sister Nahid's specialty. This used to be and probably still is my favorite cake. It's absolutely delicious and goes great with tea.*

***Nut Layer:***
½ cup semi sweet chocolate (chopped)
½ cup walnuts or almonds (chopped)
¼ cup sugar
1 teaspoon cinnamon

Mix the chocolate, chopped nuts, ¼ cup of sugar and cinnamon. Set aside.

***Cake:***

2 eggs
1 ¾ cups all purpose flour
1 cup sugar
½ teaspoon baking powder
¼ teaspoon salt
1 cup plain yogurt
1 teaspoon baking soda
1 stick of butter (softened)
½ teaspoon vanilla

1. Preheat the oven to 350°.
2. In a bowl, mix the flour, baking powder, and salt. Set aside.
3. In a separate bowl, combine the yogurt and baking soda. Set aside.
4. In a large bowl, using an electric mixer, mix the butter and 1 cup sugar until light and fluffy.
5. Add the eggs, one at a time, and mix well.
6. Add the vanilla.
7. Slowly, add 1/3 of the flour mixture, and then add 1/3 of the yogurt mixture. Continue until all the ingredients are combined.
8. Spoon ½ the batter into a greased 9-inch square pan.
9. Top with ½ the chocolate-nut mixture, spreading carefully with a spatula. Continue to layer until the mixture is all in the pan, ending with the chocolate-nut mixture on top.
10. Bake for 30-35 minutes or until the cake begins to pull away from sides of the pan.
11. Cool in the pan and then cut into squares.
12. Serve with tea.

# Macaroon Squares

*This recipe was made famous by my sister Nelofer. The squares were an instant hit at several family gatherings.*

***Topping:***
1 can sweetened condensed milk
1 teaspoon vanilla extract
1 egg
¼ cup of sugar
1 1/3 cups flaked coconut
1 cup pecans (chopped)
1 cup semi-sweet chocolate chips

1. In a large bowl, combine the milk, egg, and vanilla extract. Using a whisk beat the mixture until well blended.
2. Stir in 1 cup of coconut, pecans, and chocolate chips. Set aside.

***Base:***
1 package chocolate cake mix
1/3 cup butter (softened)
1 egg

1. Preheat the oven to 350°.
2. In a large bowl, combine the cake mix, butter, and egg. Mix all the ingredients well.
3. Spread the cake mixture into a greased baking pan.
4. Spread the topping over the cake mixture.
5. Sprinkle the remaining 1/3 cup coconut on top.
6. Bake for 30-40 minutes. (The center might seem loose after 40 minutes but it will set once cooled).
7. Remove the cake from the pan and cool completely on a wire rack.
8. Cut into small squares.

# *Cereal Cookies*

1 cup whole wheat flour
1 cup old-fashioned oats or 'Kashi Go Lean' crunch cereal
1 teaspoon baking soda
½ teaspoon salt
¼ teaspoon cinnamon
½ cup firmly packed brown sugar
6 tablespoons butter
1 cup banana puree or apple sauce
1 large egg white
½ cup raisins
½ cup chopped walnuts
½ cup chocolate chips
¼ cup ground flaxseed

1. Preheat the oven to 350°.
2. Line 2 baking sheets with parchment paper.
3. In a bowl, combine the flour, cereal, baking soda, salt, and cinnamon.
4. In a separate bowl, beat the sugar and butter with a spoon or whisk. Add the banana puree (or applesauce) along with the egg white and mix with the spoon.
5. Add the sugar mixture to the flour mixture and mix well.
6. Add the raisins, walnuts, flax seed, and chocolate chips. Mix it all well.
7. Spoon out a walnut size dough ball onto the parchment paper and repeat for the rest of the dough. Allow 1 inch space between dough balls. Bake for about 10-15 minutes or until golden brown.
8. Allow the cookies to cool prior to serving.

# Chocolate Walnut Tart

1 refrigerated ready to use pie crust
1 cup semisweet chocolate chips
1 cup walnuts (coarsely chopped)
½ stick of butter (melted)
½ cup packed light brown sugar
¾ cup dark corn syrup
3 eggs
1 teaspoon vanilla

1. Place the oven rack near the bottom of the oven prior to preheating the oven to 350°.
2. Unfold the pie crust and roll it using a rolling pin.
3. Place the pie crust into a 9 inch tart pan with a removable bottom.
4. Fold the extra pie crust into the pan and press the crust against sides of the pan.
5. Sprinkle the chocolate and chopped walnuts evenly over the pie crust.
6. Using a hand blender, mix the melted butter with the brown sugar, corn syrup, eggs, and vanilla until smooth.
7. Pour the mixture evenly over the chocolate and nut mixture.
8. Put the pan in the oven and bake for 45 minutes or until the crust is golden brown.
9. Remove the pan from the oven and allow to cool.
10. Remove the bottom of the pan and place the tart in a serving dish. Remove the sides of the pan.
11. Serve plain or with ice cream.

# ***Pumpkin Bread***

3 ½ cups all purpose flour
2 teaspoons baking soda
1 ½ teaspoon salt
2 teaspoon cinnamon
2 teaspoon nutmeg
3 cups sugar
4 eggs
2 cups fresh pumpkin puree or canned pumpkin
½ - 2/3 cups of water
1 cup oil
1 cup pecans (chopped)

1. Preheat the oven to 350° F.
2. In a large bowl combine the flour, baking soda, salt, cinnamon, sugar, and nutmeg.
3. Add the eggs, water, oil, and pumpkin puree. Stir all the ingredients until well blended. (If using fresh or frozen pumpkin puree use ½ cup of water and if using canned, use 2/3 cups of water).
4. Mix in the chopped pecans.
5. Lightly grease two 9x5" loaf pans. Pour the batter evenly between the two pans.
6. Bake for about 1 hour.
7. Cool in the pans for about 5 minutes prior to transferring the loafs to a cooling rack. Allow to cool completely.
8. Serve warm or refrigerate overnight prior to serving.

*Pumpkin bread*

## Chocolate Chip Cookies

4 cups all purpose flour
2 cups butter
1 cup sugar
1 cup packed brown sugar
4 eggs
2 teaspoons vanilla
1 teaspoon salt
2 teaspoons baking powder
5 cups oatmeal (put into blender until it turns into powder)
2 teaspoons baking soda
24 oz. chocolate chips
16 oz dark chocolate bar (finely grated in a food processor)
3 cups walnuts (chopped)

1. Preheat the oven to 375° degrees (F).

2. In a big mixing bowl, mix the butter, sugar, and brown sugar until creamy.
3. Mix in the eggs (one at a time) and vanilla.
4. Add the flour, oatmeal, salt, baking powder, and baking soda.
5. Add the grated chocolate, chocolate chips, and walnuts. Mix all the ingredients well.
6. Drop 1 big spoonful of the dough mixture on an ungreased cookie sheet, about an inch apart, until all the dough mixture has been used.
7. Bake for about 10-13 minutes.
8. Allow to cool prior to serving.

# Jams & Marmalades

# Blackberry Jam

*While attending school in Humboldt County, I learned this recipe from one of my friends. Humboldt has a large supply of blackberry bushes, and during the summer, we'd go out there with our long gloves and pick the sweet, ripe blackberries and make jam. Picking blackberries is one of the hardest tasks because you get cut up by the thorns on the branches. You also get stained by the berries so wear very dark clothing while picking blackberries. Blackberry jam tastes best with cream cheese on either toasted Afghan bread or bagels.*

3 lbs. blackberries
¼ cup of water
2 lemons
6 cups sugar

1. Thoroughly clean the blackberries by removing sticks and other debris.
2. Rinse gently and place the blackberries in a pot with the water and lemon juice. Bring the mixture to a boil on high heat.
3. Reduce the heat to medium-low and simmer until the berries are cooked and the syrup begins to thicken.
4. Add the sugar and stir until dissolved.
5. Increase the heat to high and allow to boil for 10-15 minutes.
6. Remove any foam from the top and discard.
7. Pour into warmed glass jars.
8. Seal the jars and allow to cool.
9. Store in a cool dry place or refrigerate.

# Quince Marmalade

*My mom makes this jam regularly. It's great for breakfast over toasted Afghan bread.*

3 lbs. Quince
4 ¼ cups of water
6 cups sugar
2 tablespoons lemon juice
½-1 teaspoon cardamom
½ cup walnuts (chopped in big chunks)

1. Peel the quince, remove the core and seeds, and cut in quarters.
2. In a deep bowl, add water and chopped quince. Cover the bowl and allow the quince to soak in the water overnight.
3. Separate the water from the quince in 2 bowls.
4. Place the water from the quince in a pot.
5. Add the sugar to the water and bring the water to a boil.
6. Lower the heat, add the lemon juice, and simmer for 10 minutes.
7. Stir in the chopped quince along with the cardamom and walnuts. Simmer over low heat for about 1 hour.
8. Pour the hot marmalade into warmed glass jars.
9. Seal the jars and allow to cool.
10. Store in a cool dry place or refrigerate.

***Alternative version:***
1 can of cooked quince jam (found in Afghan and Arab grocery stores)
1 teaspoon cardamom
½ cup walnuts (chopped in big chunks)
½ -1 cup of water

1. Open the can of jam and put in a sauce pan.
2. Turn the heat on medium and stir the jam.
3. Add the water, cardamom, and walnuts. Simmer for 10 minutes.
4. Pour the hot marmalade into warmed glass jars.
5. Seal the jars and allow to cool.
6. Store in a cool dry place or refrigerate.

## Apricot Jam

3 lbs. of ripe Apricots
1 ½ to 2 cups of water
1 lemon (juiced)
6 cups of sugar

1. Wash the apricots, cut in half, and remove the seeds.
2. Put the apricots in a pot with 1 ¼ cups of water and lemon juice. Bring the pot to boil on high heat.
3. Reduce the heat to medium low and allow to simmer until the apricots are tender.
4. Add extra water as needed.
5. Allow the jam to reduce and thicken.
6. Add the sugar and stir until the sugar is dissolved.
7. Increase the heat and boil for 10-15 minutes on high.
8. Pour the hot jam into warmed glass jars.
9. Seal the jars and allow to cool.
10. Store in a cool dry place or refrigerate.

## Cherry Jam

5 lbs. Cherries
3 lemons (juiced)
6-7 cups of sugar
½ cup of water

1. Wash the cherries and remove the pits.
2. Place the cherries in a pot along with the lemon juice and water.
3. Turn the heat on medium high and slowly bring the jam mixture to a simmer as you stir the cherries occasionally. Simmer until the cherries are tender.
4. Add sugar and stir until dissolved.
5. Increase the heat to high and bring to a boil. Boil for 10-15 minutes.
6. Remove any foam from the top and discard.
7. Pour the hot jam into warmed glass jars.
8. Seal the jars and allow to cool.
9. Store in a cool dry place or refrigerate.

## ***Dried Fig Jam***

2 lbs. dried figs
3 ¾ cups of water
6 tablespoons lemon juice
6 cups sugar

1. Place the figs in a bowl with enough water to cover the figs.
2. Soak the figs for at least 12 hours.
3. Drain the water from the figs and rinse them in fresh water.
4. Cut out the stem and chop roughly.
5. Place the figs in a cooking pot with the water and lemon juice.
6. Bring to a boil on high heat and simmer gently until the figs are tender.
7. Add the sugar and stir until dissolved.
8. Boil the mixture until it has thickened.
9. Pour the hot jam into warmed glass jars.

10. Seal the jars and allow to cool.
11. Store in a cool dry place or refrigerate.

## Raspberry Jam

3 lbs. raspberries
6 cups of sugar

1. Clean the berries carefully and place in a pot.
2. Heat the pot on medium heat until some of the berries begin to juice.
3. Simmer on medium low heat until the raspberries are tender*.
4. Add the sugar and stir until dissolved.
5. Increase the heat to medium high and boil for 10-15 minutes.
6. Remove any foam from the top and discard.
7. Pour the hot jam into warmed glass jars.
8. Seal the jars and allow to cool.
9. Store in a cool dry place or refrigerate.

**For seedless raspberry jam:*

- *Follow the recipe above to step 3 and then press the cooked raspberries through a sieve and discard the seeds.*
- *Rinse the pot and return the raspberry pulp and juice back into the pot.*
- *Follow steps 4-7.*

# About the Author

Nafisa Sekandari is currently living in the San Francisco Bay Area with her family. After having immigrated to the United States more than 30 years ago, Nafisa understands the need to preserve the Afghan culture and traditions for the future generations. It continues to be the intention of the author to send a portion of the proceeds of this cookbook to help the women and children in Afghanistan with needs such as education, healthcare, and nutrition. For feedback regarding the book, please contact the author at afghan_cuisine@yahoo.com.

# Appendix

## D

## F



## G



## H



## J



## K

## R



## S



## T



## V

www.afghancuisinebook.com

QUICK ORDER FORM

Web orders: www.afghancuisinebook.com

E-mail orders: afghan_cuisine@yahoo.com

Postal orders: Avagana Publishing, P.O. Box 47, Fremont, CA 94537

**Please send ___ copies of Afghan Cuisine.** I understand that I may return any of them for a full refund—for any reason, no questions asked.

______________________________________________________

______________________________________

Name: ______________________________________
Address: ____________________________________
City:_____________ State: _______ Zip:___________
Telephone:__________________________________
E-mail Address:_______________________________

Sales Tax: Please add 9.75% for products shipped to California addresses.

**Shipping by Air**

U.S: $4.00 for the first book and $2.00 for each additional product

International: $9.00 for first book; $5.00 for each additional product.

www.afghancuisinebook.com

QUICK ORDER FORM

Web orders: www.afghancuisinebook.com

E-mail orders: afghan_cuisine@yahoo.com

Postal orders: Avagana Publishing, P.O. Box 47, Fremont, CA 94537

**Please send ___ copies of Afghan Cuisine.** I understand that I may return any of them for a full refund—for any reason, no questions asked.

______________________________________________

_________________________________

Name: ________________________________
Address: ______________________________
City:____________ State: ______ Zip:__________
Telephone:______________________________
E-mail Address:__________________________

Sales Tax: Please add 9.75% for products shipped to California addresses.

**Shipping by Air**

U.S: $4.00 for the first book and $2.00 for each additional product

International: $9.00 for first book; $5.00 for each additional product.

www.afghancuisinebook.com

QUICK ORDER FORM

Web orders: www.afghancuisinebook.com

E-mail orders: afghan_cuisine@yahoo.com

Postal orders: Avagana Publishing, P.O. Box 47, Fremont, CA 94537

**Please send ___ copies of Afghan Cuisine.** I understand that I may return any of them for a full refund—for any reason, no questions asked.

_______________________________________________

_______________________________

Name: ________________________________
Address: ______________________________
City:__________ State: ______ Zip:__________
Telephone:______________________________
E-mail Address:__________________________

Sales Tax: Please add 9.75% for products shipped to California addresses.

**Shipping by Air**

U.S: $4.00 for the first book and $2.00 for each additional product.

International: $9.00 for first book; $5.00 for each additional product.

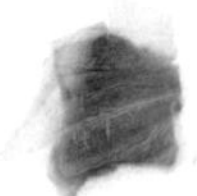

Breinigsville, PA USA
26 July 2010
242457BV00002B/2/P